THE WOMAN
WITH THE ALABASTER JAR

The Woman
WITH THE
Alabaster Jar

Mary Magdalen
and the Holy Grail

MARGARET STARBIRD

Foreword by
Rev. Terrance A. Sweeney, Ph.D.

Bear & Company
Rochester, Vermont

Bear & Company
One Park Street
Rochester, Vermont 05767
www.BearandCompanyBooks.com

Bear & Company is a division of Inner Traditions International

Library of Congress Cataloging-in-Publication Data

Starbird, Margaret, 1942–
    The woman with the alabaster jar : Mary Magdalen and the Holy Grail / by Margaret Starbird.
        p.   cm.
    Includes bibliographical references and index.
    ISBN 1-879181-03-7
        1. Mary Magdalene, Saint—Miscellanea. 2. Grail—Miscellanea.
3. Jesus Christ—Miscellanea. 4. Femininity (Philosophy)—Miscellanea.
I. Title.
BS2485.S69   1993
232.9—dc20   92–39182
                                                                                      CIP

Printed and bound in Canada by Transcontinental

20 19 18

Interior design: Angela Werneke
Editing: Brandt Morgan
Typography: Andresen Graphic Services

for Ted and our children
and for the community
Emmanuel

CREDITS

The tarot trumps of the Charles VI deck are reprinted from *The Tarot, How to Use and Interpret the Cards*, 1976, and appear courtesy of the author, Brian Innes. *Madonna of the Book, Madonna of the Pomegranate, Madonna of the Magnificat, Saint Mary Magdalen, Noli Me Tangere*, and *Road to Calvary* appear with permission from Scala/Art Resource, New York. *Saint Mary Magdalene at the Foot of the Cross* appears courtesy of The Fogg Art Museum, Harvard University Art Museums. *Derelicta* appears with permission from Alinari/Art Resource, New York. *The Penitent Magdalen* appears courtesy of the Metropolitan Museum of Art © 1978, gift of Mr. and Mrs. Charles Wrightsman. *The Hunt of the Unicorn*, Panel VII, "The Unicorn in Captivity," appears courtesy of The Metropolitan Museum of Art © 1937, gift of John D. Rockefeller, Jr., The Cloisters Collection. *La Dame à la Licorne*, panels "Sight" and "Touch," appear with permission from Giraudon/Art Resource, New York.

CONTENTS

ILLUSTRATIONS

Watermarks

Color Plates

Tarot Trumps, Charles VI Deck

ACKNOWLEDGMENTS

I wish to thank my family and friends who supported and encouraged me—especially my husband, our five children, and my parents—who suffered with me through the difficult birth throes of this book. They were a part of the quest from the beginning.

Many friends have been a continuing source of love and inspiration, especially Mary Beben. Without her help this book would not have been written. For nearly twenty years she has been my spiritual kinswoman—teacher, critic, and friend. It was she who taught me to tame some of my own "Logos" orientation and to foster my own "lost feminine." I would like to thank her for her companionship in my search for the Lost Bride.

Sue Gehringer, Anne Requa, Sandi Schneider, and Mary Findlay have shared the adventure, too. Little did we guess in the early days where the ongoing Word of God would lead us. When we first encountered the Black Madonna in 1978, we did not know the depths we would have to fathom in our quest for the neglected feminine aspect of God. She had to lead us by the hand into the dark night and the desert before we could understand that our orthodox vision of God was incomplete. I thank her now for the shortcut that spanned the abyss.

Numerous people have helped me by reading my draft manuscript and commenting constructively on it. I especially want to thank my mother Margery Leonard, my friend Mary Beben, and my editors, Barbara Hand Clow, Brandt Morgan, and Barbara Doern Drew of Bear and Company, for their careful critiques and generous gifts of time and advice. Their suggestions are greatly appreciated. Sincere thanks goes also to Bear's art director and designer of the book, Angela Werneke, and to Lee Lawson for her inspired cover painting. No one has had traveling companions more loyal and wonderful than mine.

F O R E W O R D

In one of the most illuminating and dramatic encounters in human history, Jesus said to Pilate: "For this I was born, and for this I have come into the world, to bear witness to the truth. Everyone who is on the side of truth listens to my voice." Pilate's reply to this was: "Truth? What is that?"

Pilate knew that Jesus was not guilty of any crime, yet he sentenced Jesus to crucifixion. The "truth" of Jesus' innocence was staring Pilate in the face, but he ignored it. Instead, he focused on the powers confronting him—the power of Caesar and the power of the Temple. Pilate sacrificed Jesus' life and the truth to protect himself from the religious and political powers threatening him.

There is a hard, but extremely important lesson to be learned from this encounter: Truth is not defined by political power, nor by religious conviction. Jesus was not guilty of a crime merely because Temple authorities and Pilate's sentence declared that he was, just as the sun did not revolve around the Earth merely because the Catholic Church for centuries decreed that it did. Truth is not determined by human desire, nor by human decree. Truth is the harmonization of the human mind and heart with what is.

It seems necessary to say these things because all too often power, common opinion, and tradition are taken-for-granted synonyms for truth. The Roman Catholic Church's teaching on the Holy Family is a striking illustration of this. According to this teaching, Joseph never had conjugal relations with his wife; Mary gave birth to only one child, Jesus, and she was a virgin even at the time of her death; and Jesus never married.

Throughout twelve years of Catholic grade and high schools, plus an additional twenty-three years of Jesuit and priestly education, I was presented with this delineation of the Holy Family. Steeped in this tradition, and reinforced with the notion that "with God all things are possible," I happily accepted this depiction as wholly consonant with the uniqueness of God's revelations. In this frame of mind, I looked upon any challenge to the virginity of Mary, Joseph, or Jesus as a serious affront. Very much like Margaret Starbird, who was appalled and shattered to the core by the thesis that Jesus was married, I had regarded the church's teachings on the chastity of the Holy Family as the sacrosanct "truth."

But after ten years of research into the historical origins of the church's laws regarding priestly celibacy, I finally realized that a serious bias, if not to say neurosis, permeated the church's attitudes on conjugal intimacy. This bias, originating in Gnosticism and Manichaeanism, left a resounding message that conjugal intercourse was, at best, barely tolerable and, at worst, a sinful perpetuation of evil in the world.

Marcion, one of the most persuasive of the Gnostic Christians, allowed baptism and the Eucharist only to virgins, to widows, and to married couples who agreed to refrain from sex. Marcionites regarded nature as evil, and because they did not want to fill the Earth with more evil, they abstained from marriage. Julius Cassianus, another Gnostic, claimed that men became most like beasts during sexual intercourse and that Jesus had come to the Earth to prevent men from copulating. Saint Ambrose regarded marriage as a "galling burden" and urged anyone contemplating marriage to be mindful of the bondage and servitude of conjugal love. Tatian thought sexual intercourse was an invention of the devil and felt that the Christian life was "unthinkable outside the bounds of virginity." Augustine said that nothing more brought "the manly mind down from the heights than a woman's caresses and that joining of the bodies without which one cannot have a wife." Justin Martyr was so suspicious of conjugal intercourse that he could not imagine Mary as sexually conceiving Jesus; he argued instead that Mary must have conceived while a virgin. Origen, who believed that Jesus had made a vow of perfect chastity, castrated himself.

So profoundly entrenched was this suspicion of marital intercourse that the church, starting in the fourth century, enacted laws forbidding married priests to have sex with their wives or to father children. When married priests refused to comply with these un-Christian and unethical laws, increasingly severe sanctions were imposed, including fines, public beatings, imprisonment, dismissal from the priesthood, invalidation of all priestly marriages, and papal directives ordering the wives and children of priests to be seized as slaves of the church.

My awakening to this sexual neurosis in church teaching and laws left me profoundly shaken. Was it possible that these distorted attitudes regarding conjugal intimacy had in some significant way helped to shape the church's teachings on the Holy Family? Could it be that the church's disdain of sexual intercourse had resulted in a delineation of Jesus, Mary, and Joseph that was untrue? What if, in fact, Jesus was not the only child Mary bore? In such a case, would not Mary herself be hurt by being regarded as the virgin mother of an only child? Would this not be a denial of her other children and an affront to the truth of her intimate love for her spouse? Would not this be a tremendous disservice to the Christian faith?

The Gospel of Matthew states, "While Jesus was still speaking to the people, behold, his mother and his brothers stood outside, asking to speak to him." Mark 3:31 says, "And his mother and his brothers came, and standing outside they sent to him and called him." Luke 8:19 states, "Then his mother and his brothers came to him, but they could not reach him for the crowd." Matthew 13:55-56 says, "Is not his mother the woman called Mary, and his brothers James and Joseph and Simon and Jude? His sisters, too, are they not all here with us?" And Mark 6:3 says, "Is not this the carpenter, the son of Mary and brother of James and Joses and Jude and Simon, and are not his sisters here with us?" Saint Paul in I Corinthians 9:5 says, "Do we not have the right to be accompanied by a wife, as the other apostles and the brothers of the Lord, and Cephas?" This evidence from Scripture makes it very difficult to accept the nonscripturally based assertion by the church that Joseph and Mary had no children besides Jesus and that their marriage throughout was virginal.

Mary is not the virgin mother of an only child merely because church teaching says she is. There is a truth regarding her progeny and her spousal relationship with Joseph. It is professing that truth that honors them. If, indeed, Mary had several sons and daughters, as Scripture apparently attests, then we do her no honor by believing or asserting that she gave birth to only one child and that she died a virgin.

Similarly, Jesus is not celibate merely because the church teaches that he is. There is nothing in Scripture that proves that Jesus was married, nor is there anything in the Bible that says that Jesus was unmarried, nor that he made a promise or vow not to marry.

The Jewish scholar Ben-Chorin presents a "chain of indirect proofs" to support his belief that Jesus was married. In the time Jesus walked the Earth, Judaism regarded marriage as a fulfillment of God's command to "be fruitful and multiply." Luke 2:51–52 indicates that Jesus, living under the authority of his parents, "grew in wisdom, stature, and favor before God and men." Ben-Chorin argues that it would have been quite likely that Jesus' parents, as was the custom, would have sought out a suitable bride for him, and that Jesus, like every young man, especially those who studied the Torah, would have married. Moreover, if Jesus had not been married, he most certainly would have been reproached for this omission by those Pharisees who opposed him. And Saint Paul, in presenting reasons for supporting the value of celibacy, would undoubtedly have cited Jesus' own life, had Jesus been celibate. But Saint Paul did not. Therefore, Ben-Chorin concludes, Jesus was married.

On the other hand, one has to ask, if Jesus married, why is there no specific mention of this or of his wife's name in Scripture? Margaret Starbird's answer to this is that the physical threat to his spouse's life would have been reason enough to exclude his wife's name from all contemporary written records. This explanation is very plausible, particularly in light of the severe persecutions of the earliest followers of Jesus. She goes on to say, "I cannot prove that Jesus was married or that Mary Magdalen was the mother of his child. . . . But I *can* verify that these are tenets of a heresy widely believed in the Middle Ages;

that fossils of the heresy can be found in numerous works of art and literature; that it was vehemently attacked by the hierarchy of the established Church of Rome; and that it survived in spite of relentless persecution."

Questioning the tenets of one's faith can be extremely difficult and threatening, particularly when dealing with the emotionally charged issue of the sexual identity of the Holy Family. It is far more comfortable to accept the official teaching and tradition as the sole truth. Although the Catholic Church has made numerous and wonderfully positive contributions to the development of spirituality and civilization, its attitude on human sexuality has manifested serious flaws. If these flaws have created an untrue image of Jesus, Mary, and Joseph, then it is incumbent upon conscientious Christians to do everything possible to discover the truth about the Holy Family. Such a quest will undoubtedly require sacrifice and will expose the searchers to abuse and ridicule. Courage and a profound respect for the truth are necessary virtues for this pilgrimage, as the journey is fraught with threats, allurements, and deceptions.

This book is a courageous exploration of an extremely delicate question. It attempts to discover the meaning of the Holy Grail and to restore the lost bride of Jesus. Whether or not Jesus was married has yet to be proved, and the author herself admits that her own findings, as informative and significant as they are, do not prove her thesis. But until the church can offer real proof that Jesus was celibate, those who search with their minds and hearts and souls for the truth about Jesus and his family should not be feared or scorned, but greatly commended.

Rev. Terrance A. Sweeney, Ph.D.
Sherman Oaks, California
January 1993

Rev. Terrance A. Sweeney, author of A Church Divided *and* What God Hath Joined, *holds a master's in communication arts and a Ph.D. in theology and the arts.*

P R E F A C E

Institutional Christianity, which has nurtured Western civilization for nearly two thousand years, may have been built over a gigantic flaw in doctrine—a theological "San Andreas Fault": the denial of the feminine. For years I had a vague feeling that something was radically wrong with my world, that for too long the feminine in our culture had been scorned and devalued. But it was not until 1985 that I encountered documented evidence of a devastating fracture in the Christian story. On the recommendation of a close friend who knew of my intense interest in Judeo-Christian Scriptures and the origins of Christianity, I read a book in April 1985 entitled *The Holy Blood and the Holy Grail*, which was published in the United States as *Holy Blood, Holy Grail.* I was frankly appalled.

My first impression of *Holy Blood, Holy Grail* was that the authors, Michael Baigent, Richard Leigh, and Henry Lincoln, had to be wrong. Their book seemed to border on blasphemy. At its core was the suggestion that Jesus Christ was married to the "other Mary" found in the Gospels. She is the one called "the Magdalen," the woman shown in Western art carrying an alabaster jar—the saint whom the church calls a penitent prostitute. I was not merely shocked by this suggestion, I was shattered. How could the church have failed to mention this if it were true? So important an allegation could not have been overlooked for the entire two thousand years of church history! Yet the evidence compiled by the authors of *Holy Blood, Holy Grail* suggested that the truth had been ruthlessly suppressed by the Inquisition for centuries.

Being a faithful daughter of the Roman Catholic Church, I immediately assumed that the authors of the heretical book were mistaken. But their central thesis—that Jesus had been married—gave me no rest. It haunted me. What if it were true? What if Mary Magdalen, the wife of Jesus, had somehow been deleted from the story, and what if the infant church had then continued to develop without her gentle presence?

Pondering the implications of that terrible loss to the church and to humanity became unbearable for me. In tears, I prayed about this heretical version of the Gospel. I knew that I had to find the truth. Armed with an academic background in comparative literature, medieval studies, linguistics, and Scripture studies, I dried my tears and set out to research the heresy, assuming that I would soon be able to refute its tenets. The book had touched on many areas of my own special interest and expertise: religion, medieval civilization, art, literature, and symbolism. I had taught Bible study and religious education for years, so I knew the terrain.

In the beginning, I thought that debunking the heresy would be a simple matter. I went directly to the paintings of artists implicated by the authors of *Holy Blood, Holy Grail* as having been in collusion with the Grail heresy. I examined symbols in these works, cross-referencing them with watermarks of the Albigensians (heretics who flourished in the south of France around A.D. 1020–1250), which I had found years before in an obscure work by Harold Bayley called *The Lost Language of Symbolism*. I was disconcerted to discover that the works of these medieval artists contained obvious references *in support of* the Grail heresy. Unable to refute the heresy based on their work, I continued my quest.

My research eventually drew me deep into European history, heraldry, the rituals of Freemasonry, medieval art, symbolism, psychology, mythology, religion, and the Hebrew and Christian Scriptures. Everywhere I looked, I found evidence of the feminine that had been lost or denied in the Judeo-Christian tradition and of the various attempts to restore the Bride to her once-cherished status. The more deeply involved I became with the material, the more obvious it became that there was real substance in the theories set forth in *Holy Blood, Holy Grail*. And gradually I found myself won over to the central tenets of the Grail heresy, the very theory I had originally set out to discredit.

In amassing material for this book, I have operated under the assumption that where there is smoke, there is fire. When so much evidence from so many diverse sources can be assembled to attest to a single hypothesis, there is good reason to take that hypothesis seriously. Thus, there could easily be some truth in the rumors that have persisted for two thousand years, surfacing most recently for all to see in the film versions of *Godspell*, *Jesus Christ Superstar*, and *The Last Temptation of Christ*, movies which depict the relationship of Jesus and Mary Magdalen as one of special intimacy and significance.

Of course, I cannot prove that the tenets of the Grail heresy are true—that Jesus was married or that Mary Magdalen was the mother of his child. I cannot even prove that Mary Magdalen was the woman with the alabaster jar who anointed Jesus at Bethany. But I *can* verify that these are tenets of a heresy widely believed in the Middle Ages; that fossils of the heresy can be found in numerous works of art and literature; that it was vehemently attacked by the hierarchy of the established Church of Rome; and that it survived in spite of relentless persecution.

The heresy that kept alive the other version of the life of Jesus was ruthlessly hunted down, tried, and sentenced to extinction. But the story of the Sacred Bridegroom/King of Israel proved too virulent even for the Inquisition. It kept cropping up again and again, like a sturdy vine that spreads underground and then surfaces. It appeared in places where the Inquisition and the establishment could not root it out—in the folk tales of Europe, its art, and its literature—always hidden, often coded in symbol, but ubiquitous. It kept alive the hopes of the Davidic bloodline, which was often called the "Vine."

There are several distinct possibilities regarding this heresy of Jesus' marriage. Perhaps it was true and survived because its adherents not only believed but *knew* it to be true (perhaps through some proof, such as the famed "treasure of the Templars," in the form of authentic documents or artifacts); or perhaps it was promulgated in an attempt to restore the lost feminine principle to Christian dogma, which was clearly unbalanced in favor of the masculine.

This restoration of the balance of opposites, the foundation of classical philosophy, must have been understood as necessary for the well-being of civilization. The cult of the feminine flourished in Provence in the twelfth century. Concurrent attempts of the Jewish Cabalists to restore "Lady Matronit" as the lost consort of Yahweh in Jewish mythology attest to the fact that such restoration of the feminine was considered important, indeed vital. A similar movement is afoot today in the Western world, tapping into Jungian studies in psychology, Asian understanding of yin/yang and Goddess awareness. Also significant are the numerous recent apparitions of the Virgin Mary—"Our Lady, Queen of Peace"—the only Goddess image allowed in Christianity, and her icons, which have been seen to shed tears in Christian churches worldwide. These phenomena have been widely reported in the media in recent years. The church cannot claim that there is no message. Even the stones cry out! The scorned and forgotten feminine is begging to be acknowledged and embraced in our modern age.

The loss of the feminine has had a disastrous impact on our culture. Both male and female are deeply wounded as the second millennium of Christianity draws to a close. The gifts of the feminine have not been fully accepted or appreciated. Meanwhile, the masculine, frustrated by an inability to channel its energies in harmony with a well-developed feminine, continues to lead with the sword arm, brandishing weapons recklessly, often lashing out with violence and destruction.

In the ancient world, the balance of opposite energies was understood and honored. But in our modern world, male attributes and attitudes have dominated. It is a short step from the worship of the power and glory of the male/solar principle to "son worship," a cult that too often produces a spoiled and immature male—angry, frustrated, bored, and often dangerous. Eventually, unable to integrate with his "other half," the masculine suffers burnout. The end result of the devalued feminine principle is not just environmental pollution, hedonism, and rampant crime—the ultimate end is holocaust.

This book is an exploration of the heresy of the Holy Grail and an argument for the restoration of the wife of Jesus based on important circumstantial evidence. It is also a quest for the meaning of the Lost Bride in the human psyche in the hope that her return to our paradigm for wholeness will help to heal the wasteland.

In this book, I have recorded the results of my personal search for the Lost Bride in the Christian story. I have tried to explain how she came to be lost and how devastating that loss has been for Western civilization. And I have tried to envision what would happen if the Bride were to be restored to the paradigm.

The years I have spent researching this material have taken their toll. I did not take the story lightly. I have struggled with the material in this book, wrestling with it to give it form and substance. The labor was both long and difficult. At times I feared it would turn me inside out. Doctrines I had believed on faith had to be uprooted and discarded, and new beliefs had to be sown and allowed to take root. The entire Roman Catholic framework of my childhood had to be dismantled to uncover the dangerous fault in the foundation and then the belief system carefully rebuilt when the fissure had been sealed. This process has taken seven years. At some point, I gave up being an apologist for doctrine and embarked on a quest for truth. I am excruciatingly aware that my conclusions are not orthodox, but that does not mean that they are untrue.

Many people are becoming increasingly aware of the chasm between the discoveries of modern Bible scholars and the version of Christianity taught from the pulpits of churches. I hope this book will serve as a bridge that spans this gap. While I was a student at Vanderbilt Divinity School in Nashville, Tennessee, in 1988 and 1989, I discovered that many illuminating books written by Scripture scholars lie fallow on library shelves for decades without ever being read or noticed, partly because of the dryness of their style and diction. For this reason, I decided to write in the vernacular. I have included footnotes when necessary, but basically I have told the story in a form that can be easily received and digested. A friend once told me that instead of grinding my offering of grain and baking it, I tend to dump it by the bushel into people's laps. In this book, I have attempted both to grind the grain *and* to bake it into a nourishing loaf.

In writing this book, I have taken the liberty of comparing passages in several Bibles and choosing the wordings that best expressed the meanings I was trying to convey. The Bible I have used for years and from which the majority of my quotations are taken is the *Saint Joseph New Catholic Edition* (1963), only because it is the Bible with which I am most familiar. In several cases, the text chosen was from the *New International Version* (NIV) of 1978 and is so identified. I have tried to be consistent in using the names and numbering for the books and psalms found in the Protestant canon of the Bible because these are most widely recognized.

It is my hope that this book will inspire others to begin their own personal quests for a most precious treasure of Christianity, a "pearl of great price": the Holy Grail.

The Woman
WITH THE
Alabaster Jar

MIRIAM OF THE GARDEN

This prologue, "Miriam of the Garden," is a fictional short story, a plausible setting for the rest of this non-fiction book. It is based on the Gospel narratives and cultural milieu of first-century Judea. Facts gleaned from Scripture and other contemporary sources create a reasonably accurate picture of how that story might have been—the Greatest Story Never Told.

In this fictional prologue, the Hebrew names Yeshua, Miriam, and Yosef are used for Jesus, Mary, and Joseph.

She shivered, gathering her cloak closer around her slim body. It was cool now. The blazing sun had set beyond the garden wall, beyond the Temple on Mount Sion. The fragrances of the garden lulled her, easing her taut nerves as she sat huddled on the stone bench under the almond tree. The silver of the waning moon cast shadows on the path. She rubbed her toe in the soft dust, forming gentle mounds in the loose earth.

A light step on the path startled her. She tried to discern the figure whose face was in shadow and whose form was enshrouded in a dark cloak. The man observed her for a moment in silence. Like a bird, he thought—so vulnerable. He spoke softly, trying to dispel her fear. "Shalom, Miriam. It is I, Yosef."

The slim figure before him relaxed visibly at the sound of his familiar voice. "Oh, Yosef." Her voice caught. He gazed at her with compassion. She was pale and shaken, engulfed in sorrow. He reached out his hand, an involuntary gesture spanning the fragrant darkness that separated them in the moonlit garden.

"Yosef," she whispered, "I'm not sure I can bear it. He tried to warn me, and I thought I understood." She was trembling, shaking in the darkness.

Yosef reached for her shoulders and held her firmly. He had not realized the depth of his own pain until now. Her long, dark hair gleamed in the moonlight, her eyes glistened with tears.

"Miriam," he said softly. He hesitated. Was she not distressed enough already? But he had promised his friend that he would protect her. And there was only one way: they must leave immediately, under cover of darkness. There was no telling when the authorities might come looking for her.

"Miriam, I have received a warning. We must leave Jerusalem—tonight. It is not safe for you to remain here. Pilate and Herod Antipas may be searching for you."

She turned away, gazing off into the shadows. Slowly she turned again to look at him. "You think it is necessary for me to flee?" Her whisper was barely audible.

He hesitated. "Yes, Miriam. It is the only way. I promised Yeshua that I would protect you with my life. There is no choice."

She nodded. "Yes, Yosef. I know. He read to me the words of Micah, the prophet. I understand. It is for the promise. I will do as you suggest. But what of Martha and Lazarus?"

Yosef shook his head. "I did not even tell them where we are going. I have told them that I will hide you in the city. No one is to know that we are gone until the danger is past. For now they will remain here. They will say that you are ill so that perhaps you will not be missed. We will send for them later."

Yosef had it all planned: they would travel as father and daughter, attracting as little attention as possible. No one must guess the identity of the young woman traveling at his side. The authorities would expect them to escape by sea, so the ports would be the most dangerous. Instead, he had chosen to flee by the land route across the desert. He had packed a few necessities for the journey and would rely on friends to supply their needs at their destination. They would flee into Egypt—to Alexandria.

He smiled a wan smile. Her youth and beauty were so appealing. The Magdal-eder, daughter of Sion, "the tower of the flock." She must go into the fields, to live in exile, just as the prophet Micah had warned. But through her, dominion would one day be restored to Sion. Again he marveled at his friend who had shown them the verses in Micah's prophecy telling of this exile and the ultimate return and restoration of David's royal house. He, Yosef of Arimathea, had been charged with the responsibility for her safety. He would not fail his friend.

"We will go now," he told her softly. "I have our donkeys tethered at the gate. I have spoken with Lazarus and Martha. We will send for them when the danger is past. I promise."

She knew he was right. She had known all day that it would be necessary to flee from the jealous hatred of Herod Antipas, so insecure on his throne that he could tolerate no rival. And from the Romans, too; they feared an insurrection of the Jewish nation. The hatred of the Jews for the Roman forces of occupation was intense, and their love and enthusiasm for the Son of David who had been so brutally executed could kindle a revolution at any moment. Better that she flee, lest rumors of the body's disappearance spark a suicidal con-frontation of the people with the power of the Roman legions. She understood, young as she was. Her husband had explained it all to her, holding her gently afterward while she buried her tears in the warmth of his shoulder. He had tried to comfort her, and she had tried for his sake to be brave. But she had failed, and she had seen in his eyes the anguish he felt for her.

"I am ready, Yosef. Let us go." Silently she gazed around the gar-den, breathing in the scent of lime and lilies, the dust in the air. I am leaving my home, she thought—probably forever. My brother and sis-ter, the house where we grew up, the garden where we played. The garden where I first met my Lord. Our enclosed garden. She paused, remembering.

Taking Miriam by the hand, Yosef walked slowly toward the gate, the cool dust of the path pressing against their feet in open sandals. He helped his friend's widow mount the waiting donkey and untied it. Walking slowly, his staff in his hand, he led the donkeys away from the villa. Occasionally he glanced up at Miriam. She appeared to have lapsed into an internal world of her own and no longer seemed aware of him. He walked beside her in silent communion, leading her out of the village and down the winding road, away from the home of her youth, away from Bethany and the Mount of Olives and out into the desert, their path brightly lit by the moon.

She could smell and taste the grit, windborne on the desert. Her lips were parched, her eyes burning; she kept them half closed to protect them from the blazing sun and the stinging sand. She drew her cloak closer, shielding herself from the hostile elements in a cocoon of white wool. Yosef walked silently by her side, lost in his own thoughts, occasionally seeking assurance that she was not too tired or parched—careful for her comfort, yet knowing that they must continue quickly on their way.

She sat rocking gently back and forth on the back of the donkey, her thoughts drifting again as they had off and on for days. Her reverie was unbroken by outside distractions, for the landscape was unchanging. She remembered when she had met Yeshua. She had been sitting alone on the bench in the walled garden of her home in Bethany. Her brother Lazarus had brought Yeshua into the garden and had walked with him there in the cool shade, unaware of her presence. She had heard of this man Yeshua—who had not? He was acclaimed throughout Judea. She knew how much her brother admired him. Now, seeing him, she had felt drawn to him as well. He was taller than average, with long, lean lines and beautiful hands. His hair and beard were neatly trimmed, his eyes dark and intense. But the most compelling aspect of the man was his calm assurance, an air of authority and integrity that enhanced his stature.

Then Lazarus had looked up and discovered her, silent under the almond tree. He had drawn Yeshua toward her and spoken her name. But no introduction had been necessary, because as they looked at one another for the first time, she had realized that he knew her already.

He had smiled: "Shalom."

"Peace and well-being." She had answered his time-honored greeting, and in his look she had known herself to be beautiful. She could feel it in his eyes. She knew then that she would always love this Yeshua, her brother's friend. She had looked down in confusion, blushing, her long, dark tresses falling forward to hide her face.

"I will find Martha and prepare something for your refreshment," she had murmured. And she had fled from the garden, almost tripping in her haste.

Several months later, they had married. She smiled now, remembering how surprised she had been when Lazarus had come to her with the news that he had accepted the Galilean stranger as his brother-in-law. An heiress of the lands bordering Jerusalem, she was to be the bride of Yeshua of Nazareth, born of the lineage of David the King.

The marriage had dynastic importance, uniting the families of those true friends—David, son of Jesse, and Jonathan, son of Saul. Their friendship was a story that had been told for centuries in every Jewish home. Her marriage to Yeshua was political, Lazarus had explained to her, but it was also a fulfillment of prophecy. Lazarus and his Zealot friends were convinced that the Herodian tetrarchs who collaborated with the Romans had usurped the throne of David. They were also convinced that God would send them a Davidic Messiah who would deliver the nation from the tyranny of Rome and bring about the era of peace and prosperity promised by their prophets. The stranger from Galilee had the correct genealogy; and was he not also a worker of miracles and wonders, healing the sick and casting out demons? Clearly he was God's choice. Now he must choose his bride from the tribe of Benjamin, for it was written in the first book of the Torah that the silver chalice was hidden in the sack of Benjamin. According to their inspired teachers, this meant that a woman from Benjamin's tribe would be the instrument for the reconciliation and healing of Israel.

None of this had mattered to Miriam. The elders could give any reason they wanted for their decision. They could not hear her blood singing in her veins, could not hear her heart's silent song: It does not matter why he chooses me; it matters only that I am chosen!

Pondering all these things, she had sought refuge in the walled garden, her shaded bench under the almond tree. Later Yeshua had found her there. Standing silent before her, he had held out his hand. She had looked up, hesitating, then shyly reached out to accept it. And every wound she had ever known had been healed.

They had celebrated their marriage at the house of Simon the leper. Only a few close friends and their families had attended. It was considered necessary to keep the marriage as quiet as possible lest Herod Antipas discover that an heiress of Benjamin had been united in marriage to an heir of David. Miriam had not cared that she would not be acknowledged in public as the wife of Yeshua. It had mattered only that she was the bride of the tall Galilean whose dark eyes caressed her, making her joyful, making her whole.

The wedding guests had been jubilant, believing that David's line would be restored and Sion liberated. All nations would then flock to Jerusalem to worship the Holy One in his Temple, and God's Word spoken through the Hebrew prophets would be fulfilled. The stone water jars of Judaism had today been filled with a new wine, the messianic hope for the future.

Miriam had sat quietly at the side of her husband, slim and lovely, her dark eyes shining. She had understood the political objectives of her brother and his Zealot friends, but they had not seemed relevant. All that had been important to her was the tall, handsome husband to whom she was now committed. The promise of the psalmist was tucked away in her heart: "Thy wife shall be as a fruitful vine in the recesses of your home." Amen. Shalom.

That night he had held her. He had called her "beloved," and her joy had been unfathomable. The scent of lime had drifted from the courtyard into their room on the evening breeze, and they had slept.

Yosef spoke again, interrupting her thoughts. "Miriam, Miriam.

Here, please take some water." Suddenly she was back in the present, gently brushing the sand from her eyelids. Yosef was offering her the water pouch.

"Thank you, Yosef. You are very kind."

He smiled at her. He felt a great tenderness for his queen. Her safety was his sacred trust. He had promised Yeshua. It was service gladly rendered his friend. Through her, the Magdal-eder, dominion would be restored. But for now she must go into the fields, to travail in exile, as the prophet Micah had foretold. Compassion for her wafted over him. She was chosen for this role, but how much easier it would have been had she not been chosen!

"We will be in the Nile Delta by tomorrow at nightfall," he said to lift her spirits. For days he had been worried by her long silences, hoping that she was not dwelling on the horrors of those last days in Jerusalem. He would have had her remain in Bethany with Martha after the soldiers of the Sanhedrin had led Yeshua away, but she had insisted on matching her husband's footsteps all the way to Golgotha.

Several other women had remained with her all day, offering support as she had stood near the cross. Still the cruelty of that Roman execution must surely have caused a great open wound in her heart. Like the thrust of the centurion's spear into the side of Yeshua that caused his death, Yosef thought wryly. His friends had hoped they could revive him after taking him from the cross before sundown, but it had been too late. Could Yahweh not have intervened? Somehow he had let his plan be thwarted by a Roman centurion with a long spear. Or was it *men's* plans that had gone awry? In any case, Yeshua had died from his wounds. Now their only hope for the kingdom of God on Earth seemed to rest with the exhausted woman riding his donkey, sipping from his leather water bottle, and trying to protect her face from the scorching sun of the desert. She is the hope of Israel, he thought, for she carries his child.

Miriam drew her cloak in closer, trying to find shelter from the relentless blaze of the sun. She could taste the sand in her mouth, feel its sting on her face. Her lips were cracked and swollen.

A wave of tenderness touched Yosef as he gazed at her. How he prayed for God's blessing in granting this woman a healthy child, the fruit of her marriage to Yeshua. The promises of the prophets that the Lord would restore the throne to the House of David must someday be fulfilled. "A shoot from the rod of Jesse," Isaiah had foretold, would be a just and compassionate ruler who would bring about the peaceful kingdom of God's rule on Earth. They had had such high hopes! What a shock it had been to see Yeshua led away to his crucifixion, struggling under the grotesque burden of the heavy crossbar, falling and trying to rise to continue his way through the streets of Jerusalem. All their dreams had been dashed as the Roman soldiers had nailed the Son of David to the cross; their horror had been magnified as the centurion thrust his lance, ripping open Yeshua's side and piercing his heart. Now the hope of Israel's nationalists rode astride a donkey across the parched wasteland of the Sinai, enshrouded in sorrow and a white cloak.

"Miriam, surely you must be uncomfortable from these long hours of riding. Shall we stop to rest?" Yosef broke the silence.

She smiled wanly at him, sensing his concern but not really caring about her physical discomforts. Pain no longer penetrated her consciousness. The separate sufferings of their long journey had subsided into one low, all-encompassing ache.

She slipped back into her reverie, lulled by the eternal sway of the donkey's slow gait through the endless desert dunes. She had known it was a dynastic marriage. She had not expected that Yeshua would look at it in any other light. She smiled now, remembering his tenderness, his gentle concern for her shyness. She could not face the bitter memories of those last days. He would not have wanted her to relive that agony and horror. Instead, her thoughts drifted back to earlier days. They had not had many opportunities to be together. "I cannot tarry, Beloved," he had said. "The people are wounded and oppressed. They are crippled and blind. They think that God has abandoned them in their misery. I must go back into the streets to bind up their wounds and heal their broken hearts." And she had let him go.

At first he had seemed surprised at his power to heal. He had told her once of feeling the power go from him when someone had touched his robe. He had understood that it was not *his* power, but the power of God that flowed through him. It was in his words, in his mien. His inspiring presence had captivated his friends and lured the multitudes.

She had been deeply grateful when he returned to Bethany after weeks and sometimes months traveling to remote corners of Galilee and Judea. It had been enough for her to sit at his feet, drinking in his words and his presence, occasionally catching his eye or a smile. She could not tear herself away, but sat mute, basking in his light. Once her sister Martha had been angry because all the tasks of organizing a meal for the large group of disciples had fallen on her shoulders. Yeshua had understood and had calmed Martha with a soft word, but Miriam had felt guilty and had torn herself away to help her sister with the household tasks.

In the last few months, Yeshua had talked to her several times about his impending death. The people had begun to say that he was the awaited Messiah, the Son of David. They had begun thronging the streets, waving palm fronds as a sign of the Messianic promises of Micah and Isaiah. He knew that the Roman authorities would not be able to tolerate turmoil among the masses and that the eruption was inevitable. A confrontation with the tetrarch and the Roman governor would lead to civil unrest and bloodshed. He must turn himself over to the Romans before street clashes occurred in which the innocent might be injured. Yeshua had told Miriam of Isaiah's prophecy of the suffering servant. He had tried to warn her. Then he had taken her into his arms to comfort her, and her pain had been assuaged.

Now something jogged her memory. The psalm—of course! Now she remembered why she had been so appalled when she had seen the Roman soldiers casting lots for the robe of Yeshua as he hung dying on the cross. It was all in the psalm. It had been told for centuries: "My God, my God, why hast thou forsaken me? . . . they have pierced my hands and my feet . . . and for my vesture they cast lots." The words seared her mind as she remembered the details of the crucifixion on Golgotha. A moan escaped her, but when Yosef looked up, something in her face prevented him from speaking. He would not intrude. She seemed beyond comfort, beyond a threshold of anguish, where she could not be reached.

He knew, she thought. He always knew. That is why he showed me those Scriptures—so that I would know that the prophecies of our people were fulfilled in him and so that we would all recognize that he was sent by God. She had not fully understood it until now. God is so often scorned and tortured in his prophets. God is wounded: "With a rod they strike the face of the Ruler of Israel," says Micah. In suffering crucifixion, Yeshua had shown them an extreme dimension of God's woundedness.

Her husband had often quoted to her from the Song of Songs, the hymn of the Sacred Marriage. "For love is stronger than death," she remembered now. Of course! In the ancient cults indigenous to their land, the bridegroom god dies a sacrificial death and is buried. Then later, after three days, he is resurrected amid shouts of joy by the people who have awaited his return. He has brought fertility to the land, renewing it through death and rebirth.

One evening while Yeshua was reclining at the table with his friends, Miriam had taken an alabaster vial of spikenard, part of her dower, and poured it over his head. Was not the Son of David the Anointed One, the true king of Israel and God's chosen Messiah? Yeshua had not objected to her action. His disciples had murmured that Miriam was wasting the costly unguent, but Yeshua had understood. In anointing him, she had proclaimed him both king and bridegroom. "She has anointed me for burial," he had said. She had wept then, kneeling before him and wiping her tears from his feet with her hair.

Even now, she could still feel the tenderness in his gaze. Tears began to well up in her eyes, and a heaviness enshrouded her heart. I must try not to think of the sad times, she thought. Eventually she dozed off again, still riding the donkey led by Yosef.

After nearly a month's journey, they reached their destination one evening as the shadows began to lengthen in the cosmopolitan city of Alexandria. Yosef led the donkey through the winding streets of the teeming city, seeking the Jewish sector. Infinite relief and gratitude gave him renewed energy. They were safe at last. They would not be recognized in this foreign city, far from the clutches of the usurpers of Israel's throne, far from the high priests of the Temple of Jerusalem and the Roman governor of Judea. The true queen and her son, heir to David's throne, would find haven here. One day, through her, dominion would be restored to Sion, just as Micah had promised. But for now, she was safe in exile. The "Scepter" from the branch of Jesse would be preserved and the line continued through her son. Eventually the heir of David would return to Jerusalem and claim the throne of his birthright. His rule would be established, as God had promised through the prophets. So Yosef of Arimathea believed. He found the street he was seeking, turned toward the house of his friend, and knocked on the door.

Miriam awoke to the sound of pounding. It reverberated in her ears like the sound of the hammer pounding the great iron nails into the wrists of Yeshua. "No! No!" she cried out, turning violently from the noise in her half-sleep. She fought to open her eyes, to escape the memories. The light from outside filtered through the cracks around the door, proclaiming the morning. She was grateful. Now she was fully awake.

Her body was heavy with child, her arms and legs still thin. Months had passed since her journey across the desert. She had been well cared for by the friends of Yosef. They had tried to make her comfortable, tried to console her for her loss of family and homeland.

Mostly she sought solace in her own thoughts. She was happiest alone. The sights and smells of Alexandria did not entice her. She was content to sit in the garden watching the little birds, gazing at the bright blossoms. Often she helped with the cooking or weaving, chores she enjoyed. She was content. She tried not to think of Jerusalem, of the traumatic days before her departure. It did not help; it only lay heavy on her heart.

Now and then she wondered about the empty tomb of Yeshua. What did it mean? She was still confused . . . and hurt. She had wanted to anoint his body as tradition expected. She had gone at first light on the morning following the Sabbath to the tomb in Yosef's garden where they had laid Yeshua's tortured body. But he had not been there. In terror, she had fled from the empty tomb.

In her confusion she had stumbled and fallen. When she had gathered herself together and looked up, she had seen the gardener walking toward her. Desperate, she had called to him, begging him to tell her where they had laid Yeshua's broken body. But then she had suddenly realized that it was Yeshua himself who approached! With a joyful cry, she had thrown herself into his outstretched arms. He had gently helped her to her feet, smiling at her but at the same time shaking his head. "Do not cling to me," he had said. Then tenderly but firmly he had loosened her grasp, and with a sign of farewell he had faded away as suddenly as he had appeared. She had been left to stare blankly around the empty garden.

The child within her stirred. Looking down, she smiled. It would not be long now. Her son would be strong and beautiful, the fulfillment of the prophecies: a just and righteous ruler, the anointed Son of David. He would be a most special son, the hope of Sion. She would wait patiently for God's words to be brought to completion. Awkwardly she rose from her bed and dressed for the day, secure in her faith.

Miriam's labor was long and difficult. Several times she nearly gave herself away, then forced herself to return. Time dragged on. Finally, after long hours had passed and day had turned to night and then back to day, she began to be afraid and called out. The midwife bathed her forehead with cool water, gave her encouragement, whispered promises to her. She was exhausted. It *must* be finished, she anguished, yet it went on, wave after wave. Several times she saw the worried women exchange glances. They were losing heart, too. They had done all they could. Now she was alone and exhausted.

"My God, My God, why hast thou forsaken me?"—the words of Yeshua from the cross echoed in her ears. She felt herself slipping away from the pain, escaping at last. Then she thought she saw Yeshua reaching out to her, smiling at her, taking her hand in his. Gradually his strength began to seep into her, restoring life to her body and giving her renewed energy. "You must go back," he said, "for our child."

His smile renewed her strength. A wave of pain met her as she returned to the threshold of consciousness. But she was no longer afraid. He was with her—had never left her. She understood now. He was as close to her as the beating of her own heart: "For love is stronger than death."

A last wild moment of abandon to pain, and then it was over. The midwife held up the child, finally freed from the mother's womb. She smacked the baby on the back, and it let out a small, sharp cry of surprise.

"Your child, Miriam. Your baby lives," the midwife announced, jubilant after the long, desperate hours. "A beautiful baby. A daughter."

Shock and disbelief slapped Miriam across the face. It *can't* be, she thought. What about the promises, the prophecies? There must be some mistake. It cannot be a daughter. The Son of David, the Scepter of Israel, cannot be a girl! In her exhaustion and confusion, she lapsed into unconsciousness.

Hours later she awoke. The room was fresh and clean, all traces of the difficult birth removed. Someone had brought red roses from the garden and placed them in a vase on the table near Miriam's bed. A woman was standing quietly beside her, holding a small bundle. What was it? What did she want? Miriam could not remember where she was. She looked up at the woman in confusion, smiling wanly.

"Miriam, I have brought your child. You must look at her. She is perfect, a beautiful baby. Do not turn your face away from your child." The woman seemed distressed. Her concern for the baby was real. A child whose mother scorned it rarely lived.

Miriam gazed at her for a moment in silence, remembering. The cloud of pain and disillusionment began to envelop her again. She turned her head away and stared at the wall.

"Miriam, only look at your child. See? She whimpers. She needs you. Do not forsake your daughter. Think but a moment: she is innocent. She has done nothing to offend you. Can you reject your own daughter, your own flesh?"

Gradually the words began to penetrate into Miriam's consciousness, slicing through the layers of pain. My baby—the child of my love, she thought. Now she remembered: Yeshua had wanted her to come back. He had sent her back for the sake of their child.

She turned back toward the midwife, hesitating, then slowly reaching out her arms to receive the baby. She gazed at the little red face, the tiny fingers. The infant stopped crying. Tenderness flooded Miriam as she looked at her tiny daughter resting in the crook of her arm. Each fingernail was perfectly formed.

"Before I formed you in your mother's womb, I knew you," the psalmist sang. It must be God's unfathomable will that the child of the promise was a girl. Perhaps the prophecies about the "shoot from Jesse's branch" had been misunderstood by Yeshua's friends. Perhaps it was not God's plan for her child to return to claim the throne of David in Jerusalem. Perhaps that was only the wishful thinking of men, hoping to be saved from Rome's oppression. Somehow, she knew, her baby daughter *must* embody God's plan.

"Sarah," she whispered. "I must name her Sarah . . . for Sarah believed, even when it seemed hopeless, that the promise of God would be fulfilled. I do not understand everything, but this I know: My daughter is God's answer to our prayers." She smiled down at the small bundle in her arms. A verse from Zechariah the prophet came to her: "'Not by an army, nor by might, but by my spirit,' says the Lord." Comforted, she eventually slept, her baby cradled in her arm.

Yosef came to sit by Miriam's bedside, watching as mother and infant slept. He had been taken totally off guard by the news. That the child of Yeshua might be a daughter had never once occurred to him. His belief in the literal fulfillment of prophecies for the restoration of Sion had not left room for doubt. But the child was a girl! She could not lead the armies of the Lord into battle against the forces of Rome. They would have to resort to other plans.

Yosef pondered the dilemma. The other plans would not include Miriam and her daughter. But still, he had promised Yeshua he would protect them. The friends of Yeshua would not accept Miriam now that her child had proved to be a daughter. They would never understand. There was no point in even telling them, risking exposing her whereabouts. She was safer here in Alexandria, dwelling in total obscurity. Let them forget her. Let them preach the kingdom of the Messiah without her.

He had heard of a land across the Mediterranean Sea where grass and trees grew in profusion, where snow covered the fields in winter, and where the grit of the desert sands would be a mere memory. Perhaps he should take the child to Gaul, he thought. The "vine of Judah" could flourish there, safe from the sorrows of oppression. Yosef looked down at the sleeping mother and her child. Yes. Surely they would travel on and make a new home.

It was said that it was always green in the land beyond the sea and that flowers bloomed there all year long. The God of Jacob, the Holy One, would lead them to the place when it was time to plant his vine in a new garden. Yosef smiled for the first time in days. The vine of Yeshua and the vine of Miriam—their descendants would flourish in the fertile land beyond the sea. And from there, they would one day return to Sion to reclaim their heritage, as the psalmist had promised. Like their ancestors who returned from captivity in Babylon, they would be rescued from exile: "Those that sowed in tears shall reap rejoicing. Although they go forth weeping, carrying the seed to be sown, they shall come back rejoicing, carrying their sheaves." Amen. Shalom.

Waves toss the boat,
merciless waves
slap its sides,
splash the riders of the deep
with brine.
They cling to one another
in the dark,
chant ancient litanies
to the Holy One
in their native tongue.

Yosef, watchful guardian,
questions the guidance
that bade him sail.
With heavy heart
he shields the woman and her child
from slash of waves and wind.
They show no fear,
trusting in their God.
What courage, what strength
imbue this woman
whose faith has brought her
to this moment of utter darkness.

Gradually the storm subsides.
The winds abate,
the waves, tamed,
now rock the vessel gently
like a cradle.
Serene on the breast of the deep
they sleep,
watchful Yosef standing guard,
custodian of the Sangraal,
the Holy Grail.

Now his cloak is dry.
Crystals of salt form tiny stars
as the summer sun
dries away the water's spray
that hours since
threatened to engulf them.
His eyes burn and sting
from sleep unslept
and from the bitter salt.
What does he see?
A faint shadow
there on the horizon?
A vision—pain induced?
Or land?

He awakens his friends,
points north across the sea.
"Look—our God is with us.
We have found the promised shore!"
Maximus and Lazarus retrieve the oars
abandoned in the storm.
They begin again to row.

White beaches glisten
beneath an azure sky.
Cypress, citrus, bright wildflowers
delight their eager eyes.
The men leap into the shallows
and drag their ark ashore.

A tiny smile now flickers
on Yosef's sunburned face:
he remembers Noah on Mount Ararat.
"We have survived the terrors of the night.
My sacred charge is safe at last—

the Sangraal, holy vessel
of Jesse's root and Judah's vine,
to be planted now
beside a nurturing stream.
Surely the Shepherd of Israel
Has found for us green pastures."

He helps the queen alight.
Her sandals in her hand,
she wades through shallow water
to crystal sands.
Regal she stands,
breeze stirring in her hair.

Her child is safe
and free at last—
Martha and Lazarus, too.
Fled are terrors of tyranny
and the sea's caprice.
Peace and joy envelop them.

She gazes tenderly at the daughter
born in desert exile.
"Out of Egypt I called my child."
Sarah.
God's choice was not a son
to carry arms in battle,
scion of David's house and Judah's tribe,
strong lion to crush Rome's brutal fist
and claim the royal throne.
No. God chose
this time a daughter.

What they sowed in tears,
they shall reap rejoicing
and they shall come home,

bearing their sheaves.
"And you, O Magdal-eder,
Tower-Stronghold of daughter Sion,
through you shall it come.
The former dominion shall be restored . . .
But for now you shall dwell in the fields . . .
and from there you shall be rescued." (Mic. 4:8–10)
Shalom. Amen.

CHAPTER I

THE LOST BRIDE

Based on a fourth-century legend preserved in Old French, Mary Magdalen is said to have brought the "Sangraal" to the southern coast of France.[1] It was asserted in later legends that this Sangraal was the "Holy Grail"—a chalice. In fact, it was said in later versions to have been the very cup from which Jesus drank at the Last Supper on the night of his arrest.

The Grail was revered as one of the most holy relics in all of Christendom. But sadly, according to the legends, it was somehow lost and has remained hidden up to the present time. The king is wounded and crippled, so goes the myth, and the kingdom has become a wasteland because the Grail is lost. The story promises that when the sacred vessel that once contained the blood of Christ is found, the king will be healed and all will be well. Is there anyone in Christendom who has not heard of the search for the Grail, anyone who has not sorrowed for its loss?

Some of the later European legends say that Joseph of Arimathea caught the blood of the dying Jesus in a chalice and brought it to Western Europe by boat during the early persecution of the followers of Jesus in Jerusalem (A.D. 42). One chronicler preserves the story that Joseph of Arimathea brought two cruets containing the blood and sweat of Jesus to Glastonbury in southwest England along with a staff of hawthorn that sprouted and bloomed when it was planted in English soil—the flowering staff. Other sources relate that Joseph carried the sacred Sangraal to the Mediterranean coast of France.

These various legends have given rise to numerous works of poetry through the centuries, many linking the Grail to King Arthur and his Round Table of knights who searched for the sacred chalice throughout Europe. The bottom line of all the lore is that the Grail is holy and that it is worth searching for, that it is lost or hidden, and that it will heal the wasteland if ever it is found. All are agreed that the Grail is a Christian relic, holy because it was touched by Jesus himself. It is the most sacred and most elusive artifact in all of Western civilization.

But, interestingly enough, the Roman Catholic Church has always been less than enthusiastic about the Grail and its legends. It has been suggested by Arthur E. Waite and other students of the subject that the Grail mystery and its adherents provide an alternative to the orthodox version of Christianity and that the priesthood of this "other" Christianity derives its authority directly from Jesus himself without sanction of the church.[2] No wonder, then, that the church tried to suppress the Holy Grail and its legends!

The Faith of Our Fathers

Any version of Christianity that provides an alternative to the doctrines of the orthodox church would be considered anathema. That is the definition of heresy. The question of heresy does not hinge on truth, but rather on whether or not the doctrine is in line with the official statement of the faith. Those who have been brought up in orthodox Christianity have been carefully taught to accept its doctrines on faith and have always assumed that these doctrines must constitute the one true version. However, there were several parallel versions of Christianity from the very beginning, each with its own beliefs and interpretations of the Gospel message. Over the centuries, the message of Jesus was institutionalized. Doctrines were gradually developed that did not always reflect the faith of the early Jewish Christians of first-century Palestine.

The official version of Christianity, which gradually evolved and was articulated by church councils of the third and fourth centuries A.D., was based on the consensus of the Christian elders present at the council, often with pressure from the reigning Roman emperor or other political factions. These councils voted on the articulation of doctrines such as the nature of the Trinity, the divinity of Jesus, the virginity of Mary, and the nature of the Godhead itself. They decided which scriptures from the Jewish canon were to be considered canonical by Christians and which gospels and epistles of the early church were to be included in the Bible. It was these patriarchs who decided which gospels reflected the authentic teachings and biography of Jesus and which letters of Paul and of the early church leaders should be included among the official Scriptures.

One criterion for selection into the official canon of Scripture was that a writing must be the authentic work of one of the Apostles of Jesus. On this basis, the Gospels of Matthew and John and the Book of Revelation (called the "Apocalypse of John") were proclaimed canonical, although recent scholarship suggests that in all likelihood none of the books was actually written by an Apostle of Jesus. In fact, a number of scholars consider it unlikely that any of the writers of the four Gospels ever knew the historical Jesus of Nazareth at all! In addition, there is evidence that portions of the four Gospels were deleted, added, and perhaps even censored over the centuries. It is hard, in light of these facts, to view the existing canon of Scriptures as the only possible version of the Word of God.

The official version of Christianity that was articulated by the early church councils is the same one that has been handed down through the centuries: the so-called "Faith of our Fathers." This is the orthodox version, but it is not necessarily the one and only version of the Christian faith. Nor is it necessarily true. This is the question we want to examine: Is there another story of Jesus that might be closer to the truth than the version propagated by the church during the Middle Ages before the Protestant Reformation? Was there an alternative version of Christian doctrine? Could there have been an "alternative church"? If so, what were the tenets of its faith? And what was its relationship to the early Christian message and to Jesus himself?

The Sangraal

Medieval poets writing in the twelfth century, when the Grail legends first surfaced in European literature, mention a "Grail Family," presumably the custodians of the chalice who were later found unworthy of this privilege. A connection is sometimes drawn by Grail scholars between the word *sangraal* and *gradales*, a word that seems to have meant "cup," "platter," or "basin" in the Provençal language. But it has also been suggested that if one breaks the word *sangraal* after the *g*, the result is *sang raal*, which in Old French means "blood royal."[3]

This second derivation of the French *sangraal* is extremely provocative, and perhaps enlightening. Suddenly one is faced with a new reading of the familiar legend: Instead of a cup or chalice, the story now states that Mary Magdalen brought the "blood royal" to the Mediterranean coast of France. Other legends credit Joseph of Arimathea with bringing the blood of Jesus to France in some kind of vessel. Perhaps it was really Mary Magdalen, under the protection of Joseph of Arimathea, who carried the royal bloodline of *David the King* to the Mediterranean coast of France.

Who was this Mary, known to the early Christians as "the Magdalen"? And how could she have brought the blood royal to France? Could it be that the royal blood was carried in an "earthen vessel" (2 Cor. 4:7)? What if that earthen vessel was a *woman*? Perhaps this Mary was actually the wife of Jesus and brought *a child of his* to Provence!

Both of the New Testament genealogies of Jesus insist that the charismatic teacher was descended from King David, and the messianic promises to Israel are all specifically tied to the royal blood of her Judaic princes descended from the "root of Jesse," the father of King David. The wife of Jesus, if she bore him a child, would have been quite literally the bearer of the Sangraal, the royal bloodline of Israel.

The quest for the Holy Grail is a mystery that is centuries old. Clues that link Mary Magdalen with the Sangraal of the ancient legends abound in the art, literature, and folklore of the Middle Ages, as well as in the unfolding events of history and in Scripture itself. Many of these clues will be discussed in the following chapters, in an attempt to show that the Bride of Jesus was perhaps accidentally left out of the story as a result of political turmoil in the province of Israel following the crucifixion.

I know of no way to prove beyond a doubt that the "other Mary" was the wife of Jesus or that she bore a child of his bloodline. But it *is* possible to prove that belief in this version of the Christian story was widespread in Europe during the Dark and Middle Ages and that it was later forced underground by the ruthless tortures of the Inquisition. In our search, we must identify and examine the evidence of the alternative church, the "Church of the Holy Grail," found in fossils and symbols in European art and literature and in the New Testament Gospels themselves.

Who was Mary Magdalen?

Our first step will be to establish the identity of the "other Mary" found in the four Gospels. There is strong evidence to suggest that Mary Magdalen can be identified as Mary of Bethany, the sister of Martha and Lazarus mentioned in the Gospels of Luke and John. This gentle Mary sat at the feet of Jesus while her sister, Martha, bustled around serving their guests (Luke 10:38–42), and she later anointed Jesus with nard (John 11:2, 12:3).

Biblical references to Mary "Magdalen" include the information that she was one of the women who accompanied Jesus after he healed her of possession by seven demons (Luke 8:2, Mark 16:9). She is also reported to have been one of the women at the foot of the cross (Mark 15:40, Matt. 27:56, John 19:25) and one of the women to arrive at the tomb at first light on Easter morning (Mark 16:1, Matt. 28:1, Luke 24:10, John 20:1–3). The Gospel of John says that she came alone to the tomb and encountered Jesus, at first believing him to be the gardener. She even reached out to embrace him when she recognized him, calling him "Rabboni," an affectionate form of the word *Rabbi*. Obviously, this Mary called "the Magdalen" was an intimate friend and companion of Jesus.

The Western church has an old and very strong tradition supporting the suggestion that there was only one cherished friend of Jesus called Mary. The biblical Song of Solomon, often interpreted in the Judeo-Christian tradition as being an allegory of God's love for his people, was immensely popular among Christians during the Middle Ages. Saint Bernard of Clairvaux (1090–1153), in his sermons on the Canticle of Canticles (Song of Songs), equates the bride of the song symbolically with the church and with the soul of each believer. The prototype he selects to illustrate this "Bride" of Christ is Mary, the sister of Lazarus who sat at the feet of Jesus absorbing his teachings (Luke 10:38–42) and who later anointed his feet with nard and dried them with her hair (John 11:2, 12:3). But Saint Bernard also says repeatedly in his sermons that it is possible this Mary of Bethany is the same as Mary Magdalen.

Nine hundred years before Saint Bernard, a Christian theologian in Alexandria named Origen (circa A.D. 185–254) equated Mary Magdalen specifically with the Bride in the Song of Songs. This association was broadly accepted and cherished in the Middle Ages.

The Gospel of John clearly identifies the woman who anointed Jesus with her precious unguent as the sister of Lazarus (John 11:2), and French tradition explicitly calls the Magdalen "the sister of Lazarus." The Roman Catholic Church does not even have a feast day for this Mary of Bethany, although Martha's feast day is celebrated and that of Lazarus is still honored on the Anglican calendar. One would expect the church to celebrate this "favorite sister" by honoring her with a feast as it does for the other friends of Jesus. There is a feast day for Mary Magdalen celebrated July 22, exactly one week before the feast of Martha. It seems natural and correct to give the more important of the sister-saints the prior feast day.

For centuries the official liturgical Scripture passage of the Roman Catholic Church on the feast of Mary Magdalen was read from the Canticle of Canticles, which by association equated the Magdalen with the black bride described in the song. In the sixth century, Pope Saint Gregory I proclaimed that Mary Magdalen and Mary of Bethany were the same person: "We believe that the one that Luke calls 'sinner,' that John names 'Mary' is the same out of whom, according to Mark, 'seven devils were expelled.'"[4]

The Sacred Prostitute

While two Gospels, those of Mark and Luke, maintain that Mary Magdalen was healed by Jesus of possession by seven demons, nowhere does it say that she was a prostitute, and yet this stigma has followed her throughout Christendom. The original story of the anointing of Jesus at Bethany by the woman with the alabaster jar may have been misinterpreted by the author of Luke's Gospel writing nearly fifty years after the event. The anointing performed by the woman at Bethany was similar to the familiar ritual practice of a sacred priestess or temple "prostitute" in the Goddess cults of the Roman Empire. Even the term *prostitute* is a misnomer. This term, chosen by modern translators, is applied to the *hierodulae*, or "sacred women" of the temple of the Goddess, who played an important part in the everyday life of the classical world. As priestesses of the Goddess, their importance dates back through the centuries to the Neolithic period (7000–3500 B.C.), back to the time when God was honored and cherished as *feminine* throughout the lands that are now known as the Middle East and Europe.

In the ancient world, sexuality was considered sacred, a special gift from the goddess of love, and the priestesses who officiated at the temples of the love goddesses in the Middle East were considered holy by the citizens of the Greek and Roman empires. Known as "consecrated women," they were held in high esteem as invokers of the love, ecstasy, and fertility of the Goddess. At some periods of Jewish history, they were even a part of the ritual worship in the Temple of Jerusalem, although some of the prophets of Yahweh deplored the influence of the Great Goddess locally called "Ashera." The discov-

ery in Israeli archaeological digs of virtually thousands of figurines of
the Sumerian/Canaanite love goddess (Inanna, Astarte), holding her
breasts cupped in her hands, has convinced experts that the worship
of the Hebrew version of this goddess was commonplace in ancient
Israel. The priestess of the love goddess was a familiar sight in every
city of the Roman Empire, including Jerusalem.

In the Gospel context, the woman with the alabaster jar of unguent may have been one of these priestesses. But curiously, Jesus does
not seem to have been at all affronted by her action when she anointed
him. He even told his friends gathered at the banquet in the house of
Simon at Bethany that the woman had anointed him for burial (Mark
14:8, Matt. 26:12). The significance of this statement cannot possibly
have been misunderstood by the early Christian community, which
preserved this story in its oral tradition. The anointing for burial was
the enactment of a key part of the cult ritual of the dying/rising sun
and the fertility gods of the whole region washed by the Mediterranean Sea.

The anointing by the woman with the alabaster jar was familiar to
the citizens of the empire because of the cultic rituals of their love
goddess. But in more ancient times, the anointing of the sacred king
was the unique privilege of a royal bride. For millennia this same action had been part of an actual marriage rite performed by a daughter
of the royal house, and the marriage rite itself conferred kingship on
her consort.

In those remote times, up until about the third millennium B.C.,
most of the societies of the Near and Middle East had been matrilineal, with property and position passed through the mother and female kinship. In fact, among the royal houses of much of the region,
this practice continued well into classical times. Both the Queen of
Sheba and Cleopatra of Egypt ruled as dynastic heiresses. In Palestine, almost contemporaneously with Jesus, the Edomite king Herod
the Great (who reigned from 37–4 B.C.), claimed the throne of Israel
on the basis of his marriage to Mariamne, a descendant of the Has-
monian House of the Maccabees, the last legitimate rulers in Palestine.

Cults of the Sacrificed King

Vestiges of ancient matrilineal practices and Goddess worship lingered in the first century in the Hellenized Roman province of Palestine. One repository of these ancient myths and customs was the cults of the fertility gods of the region. The anointing by the woman in the Gospels is reminiscent of the love poetry connected with the rites of the "Sacred Marriage" celebrating the union of a local god and goddess. It is not impossible that the true meaning of the anointing at Bethany was the same: the Sacred Marriage of the sacrificed king. Its mythological content would have been understood by the Hellenized community of Christians who heard the Gospel preached in the cities of the Roman Empire where the cults of the love goddesses were not completely extinguished until the end of the fifth century A.D.! And in the Gospel of John, the woman—the Bride—named in connection with this anointing is Mary of Bethany.

And yet, it is always the Mary called "the Magdalen" who is pictured in Western art carrying the alabaster jar of precious ointment, and it is on her feast day that the Roman Catholic Church traditionally reads from Canticles (Song of Songs 3:2–4) the story of the Bride searching for the Bridegroom/Beloved from whom she has become separated. In medieval and Renaissance paintings, it is invariably the Magdalen we see, her hair unbound, at the foot of the cross with Mary, the mother of Jesus; and it is she who kisses the feet of Jesus in paintings of the Disposition (the removal of Jesus' body from the cross).

These paintings recall for us the mythologies of several pagan sun/fertility gods (Osiris, Dumuzi, and Adonis) who were slain and resurrected. In each case, the bereaved widow (Isis, Inanna, and Aphrodite) poured out her grief and desolation over the corpse of her beloved, bitterly lamenting his death. Egyptian mythology, for example, relates that Isis, the Sister-Bride of Osiris, prayed over his mutilated body and conceived his son Horus posthumously. In each cult it is the *Bride* who laments the death of the sacrificed god. In poetry used in the cultic worship of the goddess Isis, some lines are identical with those found in Canticles and others are close paraphrases.[5] More recently, scholars have noticed similarities between the erotic imagery of Canticles and the love poetry of ancient Babylon, Sumer, and Canaan. The evidence has been discovered on cuneiform tablets in ancient temples and archives in this century.

The Lost Bride of the Christian tradition rests just below the surface of these more ancient myths and stories. There is a very old tradition identifying Mary of Bethany with Mary Magdalen in the Western church, and in medieval art this woman is also identified with the Sister-Bride of the ancient mythologies.

The concept of the Sister-Bride of these myths is extremely important to our story. The Bride, the moon or Earth goddess of antiquity, was the spouse of the sun god, but she was much more than that. She was the intimate friend and partner of her Bridegroom deity, his mirror image or "other half," a feminine alter ego or "twin sister." For this reason, the symbol of the mirror is retained in the iconography of the Goddess. The archetypal Bridegroom just could not be whole without her! The relationship of these two was much more than a sexual union; it was a deep spiritual intimacy and "kinship" summed up in the word *sister*. The Sacred Marriage of the Bridegroom with the Sister-Bride was not limited to a physical passion; it was a marriage of deepest spiritual and emotional ecstasy as well.

Christians in the early church readily identified Mary Magdalen with the dark Sister-Bride in the Song of Songs found in the canonical Judeo-Christian Scriptures. In a book entitled *Venus in Sackcloth*, Marjorie Malvern examines the metamorphosis of Mary Magdalen from prostitute to counterpart/friend of Jesus through two millennia of Western art and literature.[6] In this book, Malvern shows the shift in art of the twelfth century, which began to depict Mary Magdalen as the partner of Jesus in the mode and mythology of Venus/Aphrodite and other love goddesses whose domains were fertility and marriage.

Malvern suggests that this shift was the result of contact with the love poetry of the Arab world at the time of the Crusades. She notices that this intimacy was later suppressed in the thirteenth century and that the mother of Jesus was elevated to a preeminent status that she did not enjoy in the Gospels themselves. She also notes the enthusiasm in the Middle Ages for the "passion plays" of the period and the people's particular fascination with scenes enacting the anointing at Bethany and the encounter of the Magdalen with the risen Jesus in the garden.

I believe that it was the spread of the heresy of the Holy Grail that caused this surprising transformation of Mary Magdalen from prostitute to Sister-Bride in artistic representations during the twelfth century. The Mary depicted in many of these medieval paintings was not a "repentant sinner" or a "reformed prostitute," nor was she merely a friend of Jesus. She was his beloved.

Many people may be inclined to reject the idea that Jesus was married to Mary Magdalen, the sister of Lazarus. Their reason for this is very simple: they believe that the Gospels would have told us if Jesus had been married. Yet even a close examination of the Scriptures reveals much evidence in support of this marriage. Perhaps, then, we should begin our search by looking closely at the Song of Songs, whose allegorical interpretation does not hide the intensely erotic imagery of the love poem. We will also want to examine the leitmotif of the Bride and Bridegroom in Hebrew Scriptures and in the Christian Gospels. We will continue later with the quest for the Holy Grail. But first, let us study the ancient rite of the Sacred Marriage celebrated in the lands of the Middle East and in the canticle of the archetypal Bride and Bridegroom.

CHAPTER 11

THE BRIDEGROOM

I n the cities of Judah, in the streets of Jerusalem that are now deserted, there shall yet be heard the cry of joy, the cry of gladness, the voice of the bridegroom, the voice of the bride . . ." (Jer. 33:10b–11a). The theme of the Bride and Bridegroom permeates the books of the Hebrew prophets like the leitmotif of an opera. The "voice of the bride and the bridegroom heard in the land" is a sign of blessing and joy for the entire community.

In the book of the Hebrew prophet Ezekiel (16:3–63), God found his Bride while she was yet a child, naked and abandoned. He became her mentor, dressing her, feeding her, and protecting her until she came of age, and then marrying her. But she was unfaithful. This is one underlying theme of the Hebrew Scriptures—that God is the faithful Bridegroom and that his chosen symbolic "Bride," the community of the covenant, is unfaithful.

The entire book of Hosea dwells on the love God has for his unfaithful people, reflected in the steadfast and forgiving love Hosea has for his wife, the prostitute Gomer. The Hebrew prophet Isaiah prophesies a time when God will again espouse his people and their land will be healed: ". . . as a bridegroom rejoices in his bride, so shall your God rejoice in you." (Isa. 62:5b).

The theme of the Bridegroom and Bride of the Sacred Marriage recurs often in Hebrew Scripture. One familiar but curious passage from the Twenty-third Psalm, attributed to King David, is reminiscent of the ancient time when God was identified with the role of the Bride: "You spread a banquet before me, you anoint my head with oil." This line portrays God as feminine; in the rites of the ancient Middle East, the Goddess is the Bride who anoints her chosen consort, bestowing her favor and kingship on him. She is the Great Goddess of the Neolithic cultures that preceded the Indo-Aryan invasions. Rough dates for the Goddess-worshiping civilizations of Old Europe and the Near East are 7000–3500 B.C., but the Goddess was not officially banned in the region until A.D. 500 when her last temple was finally closed.[1] Then the gracious pillared halls of her earthly abode were abandoned to become the haunts of birds, and the statues of her elegant form were trundled away in carts and smashed to oblivion.

The Hieros Gamos

We have already mentioned that in the Near Eastern religions of Sumer, Babylon, and Canaan, anointing the head of the king with oil was a ritual performed by the heiress or royal priestess who represented the Goddess. In Greek, this rite was called the *hieros gamos* or "Sacred Marriage." The anointing of the head had erotic significance, the head being symbolic of the phallus "anointed" by the woman for penetration during the physical consummation of marriage. The chosen bridegroom was anointed by the royal priestess, the surrogate of the Goddess. Songs of love, praise, and thanksgiving accompanied the couple, and following the consummation of their union, a lavish wedding banquet was celebrated in the whole city amid general rejoicing of the citizens. The feast sometimes lasted for days. The blessing of the royal union would be reflected in the continued fertility of crops and herds and the well-being of the community.

Through his union with the priestess, the king/consort received royal status. He became known as the "Anointed One"—in Hebrew, the "Messiah." The one who anointed the head of the king and spread a banquet before him—who filled his cup with blessing and was his advocate before his enemies—was, in the ancient rites indigenous to the Near East, the Great Goddess. The sacred union of her royal priestess with the chosen king/consort was celebrated as a source of regeneration, vitality, and harmony for the entire community.

This ancient practice was later reflected in the annual fertility rituals of the entire region, often enacted to celebrate the new year. In some of these cults of the Mesopotamian region, the chosen consort of the local temple priestess was ritually sacrificed to ensure the continued fertility of the land. The "planting" of the sacrificed king was understood to ensure that the crops would flourish and the people would prosper.

With the Indo-Aryan invasions (circa 3500 B.C.) came the idea of a supreme male deity whose anger and wrath must be propitiated. Through the centuries, cults based on a male god of unlimited power gradually displaced the worship of the bountiful Goddess.

In Palestine, in the wake of the patriarchal articulation of the unseen God as lord and male, prophets took over the ancient role of anointing the king, a function that had once been reserved for royal priestesses of the Great Goddess. In the eleventh century B.C., the people of Israel persuaded their God (against his better judgment, according to the scriptural account), to allow them to have a king like that of their pagan neighbors. Scripture records that Yahweh was reluctant to grant their request; he had wanted to be the sole ruler of Israel. But he relented and finally gave the prophet Samuel permission to anoint Saul (about 1020 B.C.) and later David (1000–960 B.C.) king of Israel. It should be noted that David married Michol, the daughter of King Saul, according to the ancient tradition of claiming kingship through marriage to a daughter of the royal house. In the centuries that followed, the prerogative of anointing the king was given to the priests of the Temple of Jerusalem, but it was not always so; it was once the exclusive prerogative of the royal bride.

With the advent of the supreme male deity who replaced the Goddess in the civilizations of the Near East, the role of the king as the surrogate of the deity became entrenched, just as the royal priestess had once represented the Great Goddess. A poem written about 2100 B.C. in Sumer refers to Marduk, the ruling deity of Babylon, as "the Bridegroom of my well-being."[2] The Hebrew poets and prophets adopted this image of God's intimate relationship *with his people* (Ezek. 16; Hos. 2; Isa. 54, 62; Jer. 2, 3). And in the Greek New Testament, all four Gospels are sprinkled with this Bridegroom motif with reference to Jesus.

There is a great deal of evidence in the New Testament that Jesus understood the intimate marriage relationship between God and the covenant community and that he himself consciously adopted the role of the Bridegroom/King of the people. It is clear from the Gospels that Jesus did not come to overthrow Rome's dominion. The Gospel parables include repeated references to the wedding theme, and Jesus is often represented as the Bridegroom.

Jesus the Bridegroom

The people of Palestine had long awaited the coming of a Messiah, God's Anointed One, to save them from the oppression of Roman tyranny and the illegitimate and despotic rule of the capricious Herodian rulers. The hope of many Jews was that a Davidic Messiah would come with the power to cut down the enemies of Israel; their prophets had foretold it. The purist religious community at Qumran and the politically radical Zealots lived in daily expectation that these prophecies would be fulfilled.

After the death of Jesus, interpretation of the words of the prophets shifted away from a worldly kingdom, which had been their hope, to a postponed "heavenly" kingdom in an age to come. The "suffering servant" images from Isaiah—the metaphor of the obedient Lamb of Sacrifice who would return in glory to save the oppressed—became the prevailing myth of the Christian movement in the latter half of the first century and ever after.

But Jesus himself seems to have understood his own role as that of the representative of Yahweh—as the heavenly Bridegroom of Israel. As anointed King and "faithful son," he is sacrificed for the sake of the community.

The evangelist Mark carefully sets the stage for this revelation of Jesus as Bridegroom/King of Israel. He recounts the arrival of Jesus in the environs of Jerusalem prior to the Passover. As they approached Jerusalem, Jesus sent two of his disciples ahead to Bethany to procure a "colt which no one has ever ridden" (Mark 11:2). They threw their cloaks over the colt, and Jesus rode upon its back into Jerusalem. The people spread out their cloaks and branches along the way and proclaimed "the coming kingdom of our father David" (Mark 11:10).

This event fulfilled the messianic prophecy found in the book of the Hebrew prophet Zechariah. Jesus did not just accidentally participate in this; his riding on the colt was a conscious, symbolic action by which he deliberately and irrevocably proclaimed his messianic role:

> Rejoice greatly, O Daughter of Zion!
> Shout, Daughter of Jerusalem!
> See, your king comes to you
> righteous and having salvation,
> gentle and riding on a donkey,
> on a colt, the foal of a donkey. (Zech. 9:9 NIV)

In the time of the books of Genesis and Chronicles, it was customary for the charismatic leader who came in peace to come riding on a donkey, whereas a "warrior king" rode a war-horse and came bearing arms.[3] King David arranged for his son Solomon to ride his own royal donkey to his anointing as King of Israel (1 Kings 1:33–38). Mark's Jesus proclaims his mission as King of Peace by riding the colt of a donkey on his entry into Jerusalem. But he was at the same time claiming to be the heir of David, an action of tremendous political significance. He was proclaiming the fulfillment of Zechariah's prophecy: "Your king will make peace among the nations; he will rule from sea to sea." (Zech. 9:10).

The Woman with the Alabaster Jar

Bethany is a small village located on the southeast spur of the Mount of Olives. In Zechariah 14 we find the apocalyptic expectation that when the Lord comes to save Israel from her foes, he will come to the Mount of Olives: "On that day His feet will stand on the Mount of Olives, east of Jerusalem . . ." (Zech. 14:4). This prophecy elevated the Mount of Olives to the site of messianic expectation. It was to Bethany on the Mount of Olives that Jesus returned every evening after visiting Jerusalem during the week of the Passover. And it was on this mount that he was anointed by the woman with the alabaster jar.

The story of the anointing of Jesus by the woman in Bethany is one of the most important events recorded in the New Testament Gospels. It must be extremely significant, for it is a rare event indeed that is reported in all four canonical Gospels. The story of the anointing is easily the most intimate expression of Eros/relatedness in the recorded events of Jesus' life, and for that reason alone it deserves careful scrutiny. Yet it has rarely received the recognition it deserves. What was the meaning of the action of this woman at Bethany? And isn't it likely that the woman who anointed Jesus at the banquet at Bethany was the same woman who encountered him in the garden near the tomb at dawn on Easter morning?

One evening, according to Mark 14:3, "while Jesus was in Bethany, reclining at the table . . . a woman came with an alabaster jar." The action of the woman at Bethany can be understood as a prophetic recognition of Jesus as the Messiah, the Anointed One, an action construed as politically dangerous because it proclaimed the kingship of Jesus.[4]

In ancient Israel, kings, priests, and prophets were anointed with oil to receive their authority as those "chosen" to represent Yahweh. The sacred olive oil was carefully prepared by the priests in the Temple and mixed according to a prescribed recipe with other spices: cinnamon, myrrh, sweet calamus, and cassia.[5] Its secular use was prohibited on pain of excommunication. But the woman of Bethany did not use the sacred oil of the Temple priests. She opened ". . . an alabaster jar of very expensive perfume, made of pure nard. She broke the jar and poured it on his head" (Mark 14:3–4).

"Pure nard" is believed by current scholarship to be a possible corruption of the Greek word for spikenard. The aromatic unguent was a very rare and expensive perfume from a plant that grew in India. In Hellenized Palestine, wealthy women sometimes wore a small amount of this unguent in an alabaster vial, or "alabastron," on a chain around their necks.[6] It was often a dowry item. And it was a custom to break the flask, anoint the body of the beloved deceased with its contents, and then to leave the fragments of the jar in the tomb.[7]

In addition to the accounts of the Gospels that describe the anointing of Jesus with this expensive perfume, there is one other place in Scripture where spikenard is mentioned: "For the king's banquet, my nard gives forth its fragrance" (Song of Songs 1:12). It is the Bride whose fragrant spikenard spreads around the Bridegroom/King at his banquet in the Song of Songs, the ancient song of the Sacred Marriage.

The Song of Songs

Modern research into the origin and meaning of the Song of Songs illuminates the Gospel anointing of Jesus. It is believed that the song was originally a liturgical litany for performance during rites of the Sacred Marriage (the *hieros gamos*). It is very similar to the love poetry of the ancient fertility religions practiced in Sumer, Canaan, and Egypt.[8]

The Song of Songs was widely popular in Palestine during the time of Christ. Two fragments of the song were found in Cave IV of the monastic community near Qumran (concealed circa A.D. 68). This attests to its popularity in the first century among the community that hid the Dead Sea Scrolls. A Greek translation of the song dates from 100 B.C. A noted Jewish scholar and teacher, Rabbi Aqiba (who died in A.D. 135) is quoted as saying, "The whole world is not worth the day on which the Song of Songs was given to Israel, for all Scriptures are holy, but the Song of Songs is the Holy of Holies."[9] This same rabbi objected to the widespread singing of the song in streets and banquet halls, so popular was it in Palestine during this time. The Song of Songs was considered holy and approved by Jewish rabbis because it was interpreted allegorically as a portrayal of Yahweh's love for his "Bride," the people of Israel.[10] It is possible that the rabbis retained the song as a sacred book because they believed it was composed by King Solomon. For whatever reason, it seems to have been "common domain" in first-century Jerusalem.

The Song and the Cult of the Bridegroom

Some modern scholars believe that the Song of Songs was composed as part of the Sumerian fertility rites of Dumuzi and Inanna, whose myth had been current in the ancient Near East for several thousand years. Love poetry inscribed on recently deciphered cuneiform tablets describe Dumuzi as a "shepherd" and "faithful son,"[11] epithets which were later applied to Jesus! The beloved of Dumuzi is referred to as "sister" and "bride." The king was considered a "chosen son" by virtue of the fact that the deity had "formed him in his mother's womb."[12] He was anointed for his role, which included his ritual death and burial: it was the duty of the king to be united with the Goddess, Mother Earth (Inanna). After the marriage, Dumuzi was ritually tortured, killed, and buried, ensuring regeneration of the crops and herds. The king could not be allowed to become old or weak, or to lose his strength and vitality, for the life of the people was a reflection of his virility. If his power and strength were to ebb, so would theirs.

In some rites, the tortured king was entombed and then "resurrected" after a brief period, normally three days. The poetry from the liturgy includes the lamentation of Inanna over the death of Dumuzi, the goddess's search for the missing god, and an expression of joy at his return.[13] This portion of the prevailing Bridegroom myth of the pagan cults is reenacted in the Gospel of John when Mary Magdalen encounters the risen Jesus near the tomb on Easter. And it is made visual in the Pietàs and the paintings of the Disposition, the removal of Jesus from the cross, in Christian art.

The cult of the dead and resurrected Dumuzi spread to Palestine, along with the epithets of "shepherd" and "anointed." Dumuzi was the ancient prototype of the Bridegroom. As we have mentioned, the more ancient practice in the Near East was that of a matrilineal royal priestess conferring kingship on her consort, since marriage to the representative of the Goddess was essential for such status.

These rites of the vegetation and fertility gods and goddesses were well known in ancient Israel. In Ezekiel 8:14, for example, the prophet is shown a group of Hebrew women crying over Tammuz, the Babylonian fertility deity who is identified with Dumuzi. This was understood by the prophet to be an abomination. In fact, Israel's prophets had long lamented the fact that the people were unfaithful to Yahweh, their male deity. Continually, it seemed, the unfaithful community returned to the pagan worship of Ashera (Astarte) and Baal, the local counterparts of the Babylonian Inanna and Dumuzi.[14] In the words of their prophets, the people were "whoring after false gods."

During the period of Greek influence (333–30 B.C.) and into the period of the Roman Empire, the rites of other sacrificed sun gods and Earth or moon goddesses became modified, borrowed, and confused with neighboring practices. Lines that are identical and parallel to those in the Song of Songs are found in a liturgical poem from the cult of the Egyptian goddess Isis, the Sister-Bride of the mutilated sun god Osiris.[15] Ancient carvings of Isis lamenting over the corpse of Osiris provide a model for medieval Pietàs. Various theories are available as to the origin of the love poetry of the Sacred Marriage, but it is clear that the rites of the dying and rising fertility god were current in Palestine at the time of Jesus.

The Shepherd/King and His Bride

It may be impossible to determine the exact source of the biblical Song of Songs, but its meaning is obvious: it is the wedding song of the Shepherd/King and his Bride. The rites of the *hieros gamos* were so well known in the Hellenized world that the anointing of the head of Jesus could not have been misunderstood by those who witnessed it. The author of Mark's Gospel is a master at attributing mythic importance to certain events. Calming the storm, cleansing the Temple, and other stories in his Gospel proclaim the mythic identity of Jesus through action. And the story of his anointing by the woman at Bethany is no exception.

It is clear from Jesus' response to the anointing that he understood and accepted it, and that he also accepted his mythic role as the sacrificed Bridegroom/King. Throughout the Greek Bible, we encounter references to the messianic "wedding feast," and references to Jesus as "bridegroom" are found throughout the Gospels. Numerous references to the Bridegroom and the Bridal Chamber also appear in the Gnostic gospels discovered at Nag Hammadi in Egypt in 1945, a fact that attests to the prevalence of this theme among some sects of early Christians.[16]

In Mark 2:19–20, Jesus refers to the fact that his disciples are not fasting: "When the bridegroom is taken away from them, on that day they will fast." This passage is echoed in Mark 14, when the disciples complain about the cost of the wasted perfume. Jesus defends the woman, saying: "The poor you will always have with you . . . but you will not always have me." And then he announces that the woman has anointed his body for burial, confirming the proclamation she has given of the Sacred Marriage, which includes the torture and death of the anointed Bridegroom/King.

These frequent allusions to Jesus as the Bridegroom of the fertility myth could be the creation of the Hellenized authors of the Gospels. But it is far more likely that they originated with Jesus himself, in the tradition of the Hebrew prophets who had proclaimed Yahweh as the heavenly Bridegroom of the community and the king of Israel as his "faithful son" or "servant," the anointed Messiah. The theme of the Bridegroom and the "faithful son" (terms found also, as noted, in the Sumerian and Canaanite mythologies) are repeated in the Apocalypse of John, the final book of the Greek New Testament, which was written by a Jewish author at the close of the first century A.D.

Judas and the Zealots

Perhaps the most powerful evidence that the anointing was immediately understood by those at the banquet at Bethany was the action reported to have been taken by Judas. Some modern scholars portray Judas as a Zealot, a right-wing political extremist who was hoping for the overthrow of Roman rule. It is considered likely that

Judas was a member of a militant Zionist group called the Sicarii, the "Sons of the Dagger." He must have been totally disillusioned when he realized that the heir of David did not intend to overthrow Roman dominion in Judea—Jesus had chosen the role of Bridegroom, and the Reign of God was being proclaimed as a universal wedding banquet, open to all. For this reason, Judas Iscariot went to the chief priests to betray Jesus (Mark 14:10).

It is very possible that the anointing convinced him that Jesus was not the Messiah of his expectations. The Day of Yahweh had come. The Chosen One had been anointed on the Mount of Olives, but not with the sacred oil of Hebrew ritual; he had been anointed with the perfumed unguent of a *woman*. And he had not only accepted this anointing but had defended the woman's action as a prophetic proclamation of his death and burial, just as in the ancient pagan rite of the *hieros gamos*. If Judas was a fundamentalist Zealot "zealous for the Law," he would have been appalled to see Jesus willingly assume the role of the sacrificed pagan fertility/sun god.

Obviously, the Gospel version of this story was written for Christian converts who would have understood fully the mythological content of the sacrificed god theme. These pagan rites were practiced in temples in the cities of the Roman Empire until the newly victorious Christian hierarchy banned them at the end of the fourth century A.D. But the early story of the anointing at Bethany was included in all four Gospels, indicating that the eye-witnesses who first told the story must have seen something they considered extremely important.

In Memory of Her

Throughout the Gospel of Mark, whenever someone wanted to proclaim Jesus the "Son of God" or "the Messiah" he always admonished them not to tell anyone his identity. Yet suddenly in Mark 14:9, he tells his disciples that the story of the woman with the alabaster jar would be told and retold "in memory of her." Someone, perhaps Jesus himself, must have thought that this event was so significant that it should be kept alive in the community. Why?

Denis de Rougemont suggests that when an important event is too dangerous to be discussed, it is formed as a myth and told as a story.[17] This opinion, from his book *Love in the Western World* (first published in French in 1940), could be applied to the entire myth surrounding the lady with the alabaster jar. Was the story of the anointing/ marriage rite of Jesus told as a myth because of the danger to the woman who was his wife? Was it considered safer to tell the story knowing that the people who heard it would understand the woman's intimate relationship to the Bridegroom/King?

We are talking here of the *oral version* of the story, which presumably circulated throughout the Roman Empire for nearly forty years before the author of Mark's Gospel ever wrote it down. In fact, this event was so important that it survived in several different versions in the oral tradition. And yet, while it should have been considered scandalous for a woman—any woman—to touch a Jewish man in public, there is barely a hint that the friends of Jesus were scandalized by the woman's action. Their main concern seems to have been for the immense cost of the wasted perfume, valued at a year's wages (Mark 14:5). As if it had been their personal loss!

And who *was* the woman with the alabaster jar who anointed Jesus? For centuries she has been portrayed by the church as both "sinner" and "prostitute," never Bride. Yet the church patriarch Origen (A.D. 185–254) recognized the Magdalen as the Sister-Bride from Canticles, as did the communities of early Christians living in the Roman Empire of the first century. And the author of John's Gospel calls this woman "Mary, the sister of Lazarus."

There is a very strong Roman Catholic tradition that the Apostle John was the protector of Mary, the mother of Jesus, and that after the crucifixion (presumably for safety's sake) he took her to live in Ephesus. The Gospel of John, if not written by John himself, was in all likelihood written by his own disciples (circa A.D. 90–95) in Ephesus. There is evidence in this Gospel of some important historical material about Jesus that is not included in the other three Gospels.

Surely John and the mother of Jesus were the source of that material. And although it was not recorded in the earlier Gospels, the Apostle John and Mary, the mother of Jesus, would also most surely have known the name of the woman who anointed Jesus. She was Mary of Bethany, his Lost Bride.

THE BLOOD ROYAL AND THE VINE

The Fourth Gospel says very clearly that the woman who anointed Jesus at Bethany was Mary, the sister of Lazarus. Mary Magdalen's name is not mentioned in connection with the anointing scene, but it is she who accompanies Jesus to Calvary in the Gospels, standing near the cross; and it is she who goes at dawn on Easter morning to finish the anointing for burial that she began several days before. We have examined the tradition of the Western church that Mary of Bethany and Mary Magdalen were one and the same. But why was Mary of Bethany called "the Magdalen"? Why was she forced to flee Jerusalem? And what became of the sacred bloodline she carried with her?

The Secret Marriage

I have come to suspect that Jesus had a secret dynastic marriage with Mary of Bethany and that she was a daughter of the tribe of Benjamin, whose ancestral heritage was the land surrounding the Holy City of David, the city Jerusalem. A dynastic marriage between Jesus and a royal daughter of the Benjamites would have been perceived as a source of healing to the people of Israel during their time of misery as an occupied nation.

Israel's first anointed King Saul was of the tribe of Benjamin, and his daughter Michol was the wife of King David. Throughout the history of the tribes of Israel, the tribes of Judah and Benjamin were the closest and most loyal of allies. Their destinies were intertwined. A dynastic marriage between a Benjamite heiress to the lands surrounding the Holy City and the messianic Son of David would have appealed to the fundamentalist Zealot faction of the Jewish nation. It would have been seen as a sign of hope and blessing during Israel's darkest hour.

In the novel *King Jesus* (1946), Robert Graves, the twentieth-century mythographer, suggests that Jesus' lineage and marriage were concealed from all but a select circle of royalist leaders.[1] To protect the royal bloodline, this marriage would have been kept secret from the Romans and the Herodian tetrarchs, and after the crucifixion of Jesus, the protection of his wife and family would have been a sacred trust for those few who knew their identity. All reference to the marriage of Jesus would have been deliberately obscured, edited, or eradicated. Yet the pregnant wife of the anointed Son of David would have been the bearer of the hope of Israel—the bearer of the Sangraal, the royal bloodline.

Magdal-eder, the Tower of the Flock

In chapter 4 of the Hebrew prophet Micah, we read a beautiful prophecy of the restoration of Jerusalem, when all nations shall beat their swords into plowshares and be reconciled under God. Beginning with verse 8 we find:

> As for you, O [Magdal-eder], watchtower of the flock,
> O stronghold of the Daughter of Zion!
> the former dominion will be restored to you;
> kingship will come to the Daughter of Jerusalem.
> Why do you now cry aloud—
> have you no king?
> Has your counselor perished,
> that pain seizes you like that of a woman in labor?
> Writhe in agony, O Daughter of Zion,
> like a woman in labor,
> for now you must leave the city
> and camp in the open field.

It is probable that the original references to Mary Magdalen in the oral tradition, the "pericopes" of the New Testament, were misunderstood before they were ever committed to writing. I suspect that the epithet "Magdalen" was meant to be an allusion to the "Magdaleder" found in Micah, the promise of the restoration of Sion following her exile. Perhaps the earliest verbal references attaching the epithet "Magdala" to Mary of Bethany's name had nothing to do with an obscure town in Galilee, as is suggested, but were deliberate references to these lines in Micah, to the "watchtower" or "stronghold" of the Daughter of Sion who was forced into political exile.

The place name *Magdal-eder* literally means "tower of the flock," in the sense of a high place used by a shepherd as a vantage point from which to watch over his sheep. In Hebrew, the epithet *Magdala* literally means "tower" or "elevated, great, magnificent."[2] This meaning has particular relevance if the Mary so named was in fact the wife of the Messiah. It would have been the Hebrew equivalent of calling her "Mary the Great," while at the same time referring to the prophesied return of dominion to "the daughter of Jerusalem" (Mic. 4:8).

In Old French legend, the exiled "Magdal-eder," the refugee Mary who seeks asylum on the southern coast of France, is Mary of Bethany, the Magdalen. The early French legend records that Mary "Magdalen," traveling with Martha and Lazarus of Bethany, landed in a boat on the coast of Provence in France. Other legends credit Joseph of Arimathea as being the custodian of the Sangraal, which I have suggested may be the *royal bloodline of Israel* rather than a literal chalice. The vessel that contained this bloodline, the archetypal chalice of medieval myth, must have been the wife of the anointed King Jesus.

The image of Jesus that emerges in our story is that of a charismatic leader who embodies the roles of prophet, healer, and Messiah-King, a leader who was executed by the Roman Army of Occupation and whose wife and bloodline were secretly taken from Israel by his loyal friends and transplanted in Western Europe to await the fullness of time and the culmination of prophecy. The friends of Jesus who believed so fervently that he was the Messiah, the Anointed of God, would have perceived the preservation of his family as a sacred duty. The vessel, the chalice that embodied the promises of the Millennium, the "Sangraal" of medieval legend, was, I have come to believe, Mary Magdalen.

The Vine of the Lord

Many biblical passages use the word *vine* as a metaphor for the chosen people of God: "A vine thou didst bring out of Egypt" (Ps. 80:9); "The vineyard of the Lord of hosts is the House of Israel and the men of Judah are his cherished plant" (Isa. 5:7). Several passages refer to the vine as feminine: "Thy wife is like a fruitful vine" (Ps. 128); "Your mother is like a vine planted by the water, fruitful and branchy . . . but she was torn up . . . and now she is planted in the desert . . . she is now without a royal branch, a ruler's scepter" (Ezek. 19:10–14). This transplanted royal vine is understood by biblical scholarship to refer to the royal Davidic line of Judah, the line of the princes.

The Bride in Canticles carefully tends the vines. In Isaiah 5, the rebellious vineyard brings forth wild grapes. Psalm 80 is a prayer for the restoration of the vineyard: "Take care of this vine and protect what your right hand has planted." In Mark's Gospel, Jesus tells the parable of the vinedressers, caretakers of the vineyard (Israel) who beat the servants of their master when they came to inspect the condition of the vines and then killed the master's son. No one who knew Jesus of Nazareth and who "had ears to hear" was in any doubt as to the identity of that "faithful son." He was the legitimate heir to the vineyard of Judah.

The transplanting of the Davidic "vine" would have come as no surprise to the Zealot fundamentalist friends of Jesus. They knew it had been prophesied (Ezek. 17). It had happened before, when the people of Israel were taken as slaves to Babylon. But it could also happen again. In light of the danger to the vine of Judah, the royal bloodline, it is likely that the friends of Jesus took strong and perhaps desperate measures to protect the family of Jesus. It would have been their top priority.

The Flight into Egypt

Under the conditions of the Roman occupation of Israel, the Holy Family would have been kept secret and protected at all costs by the royalist faction in Palestine. It seems obvious that after the crucifixion of Jesus, Mary Magdalen was no longer in Jerusalem. There is no mention of Mary, Martha, or Lazarus in the Book of Acts or in Paul's letters. In any case, it is unlikely that Mary would ever have been identified as the widow of Jesus. The danger would have been too great. It seems more likely that these special friends of Jesus were no longer part of the community in Jerusalem at the time Paul's letters were written (A.D. 51–63), but their departure is unexplained. If they had been part of that community following the Ascension of Jesus, their names might have been mentioned in the later New Testament works that were declared canonical.

Instead, post-Ascension references to Mary Magdalen occur only in the Gnostic Gospels (of which ancient Coptic scrolls were found in Nag Hammadi in 1945 and in other sites in Egypt), texts that confirm that Mary Magdalen was an intimate companion of Jesus.[3] The Gospel of Philip says: "There were three who walked with the Lord at all times: Mary his mother, her sister, and Magdalen, the one who is called his companion."[4] Mary Magdalen is described in this Gnostic gospel found at Nag Hammadi as having aroused the jealousy of the Apostles because she was the close companion or "consort" of the Lord, who often kissed her on the mouth.[5]

It is clear from the four canonical Gospels that Mary Magdalen enjoyed special precedence in the community of believers, since she was the first person to see and speak to Jesus on Easter Sunday, having hurried to his tomb at first light to perform embalming rites for his dead body. There are seven lists in the four Gospels that name the women who accompanied Jesus. In six of the seven, the name of Mary Magdalen is given first—ahead of Mary, the mother of Jesus, and ahead of the other women mentioned. The Gospel writers, beginning with Mark, are most likely reflecting the status of the Magdalen in the Christian community—that of First Lady.

The Coptic scrolls were hidden at Nag Hammadi in about A.D. 400 during a period in which the orthodox Christian church (having been declared the official church of the Roman Empire by the Emperor Theodosius) began persecuting and destroying the documents of sects it deemed heretical. These scrolls were preserved in jars similar to those containing the scrolls of the Dead Sea Caves near Qumran in the Judean desert. Found in the 1940s and '50s, they have opened up a whole new era of research into the early centuries of Christianity. The prominence of Mary Magdalen in the four canonical Gospels is strengthened in many of these apocryphal documents. The Coptic scrolls, many of which are second- and third-century parchments, predate the existing copies of the canonical Gospels by centuries! And, miraculously, they survived the purge by the early church, just as the Dead Sea Scrolls of the Qumran community survived destruction by the Roman legions during the Jewish revolt of A.D. 66–74 when the nation of Israel was virtually destroyed and the Christian community of Jerusalem was wiped out.

Jesus and the Zealot Faction

We have touched on the politics of the Jewish Zealots at the time of Jesus. Now it is time to address briefly the nature of the charges brought against Jesus that caused Pilate, the Roman procurator of the province, to order that he be crucified—an order that thrust his wife, Mary, into the gravest danger. For if Jesus was charged only with the blasphemy of claiming to be the son of God, as the Bible suggests, his wife would have been in little danger. But if he was crucified for sedition and for his political affiliations, as I intend to show, she would certainly have been forced to flee for her life.

There is massive evidence to support the theory that Jesus was sympathetic with the right-wing activists in Israel.[6] For one thing, several of his Apostles are known to have been militant extremists, Judas Iscariot being the man most often cited. The word *Iscariot* attached to his name is widely understood to indicate that he belonged to the aforementioned radical brotherhood of political assassins, the

Sicarii, or "Sons of the Dagger." (This epithet stems from the Latin word *sica*, a short dagger, which the men concealed in their robes. *Sicarius* means "one who murders with a sica.")[7]

Another follower of Jesus, Simon the Cananean (Qu'anan) is mentioned in Matthew 10:4. The footnote in my Bible says that *Cananean* is the root word for "Zealot." Remembering that the Gospel stories were spread by word of mouth for several decades before they were first committed to parchment, it is possible that the marriage of Cana was in fact the "marriage of the Zealots." The consonants of the two words are similar enough to cause confusion in the oral tradition. Perhaps this marriage of Cana was one of national importance to the Jews—namely, that of Jesus to Mary Magdalen. The changing of water into wine could then be understood as a symbolic imparting of "new life"—a renewed messianic hope and joy—into the stone water jars of Judaism.

Stories about the life and teachings of Jesus circulated for more than thirty years before our earliest version, the Gospel of Mark, was written in about A.D. 70. The linguistic study of folk etymology confirms that details of a story are unintentionally modified as they are passed along by word of mouth. Sometimes idioms, colloquialisms, and proper names are misinterpreted or misspelled. If Simon the Cananean means Simon "the Zealot" (about which there seems to be no doubt), then "Cana" could easily be a reference to the Zealot party as well.

It is the opinion of many New Testament scholars that the charge brought against Jesus—the charge that put his wife into so much danger that she had to flee Jerusalem—was not blasphemy but sedition. The arguments for understanding Jesus as a political figure, the Jewish Davidic Messiah who posed an acute threat to the stability of the Roman province of Palestine, are carefully outlined by S.G.F. Brandon in a book entitled *Jesus and the Zealots*.[8] The spontaneous popular movement that surged in response to Jesus and his ministry was a direct challenge to the political authority of Rome. He was accused of inciting the people to riot, and the traditional Roman punishment reserved for Zealot insurrectionists was crucifixion. In fact, during the period from A.D. 6 until the fall of Jerusalem in A.D. 70, hundreds of Jewish patriots were crucified.[9]

The crowds followed Jesus from town to town during his ministry, and once or twice the Gospels report that they wished to make him king. But the action that led to his immediate arrest by the authorities in Jerusalem was the overturning of the tables of the money changers in the Temple of Jerusalem during the Passover festival. Every year, Jews from all over the empire flocked to Jerusalem to make their offerings in the Temple. The action that Jesus allegedly took, scattering coins of the empire all over the Temple floor, was a radical attack on the religious establishment of the Temple priests and Sadducees, the ruling elite who collaborated with the Roman authorities to preserve peace and order in the province.

The desert community that authored many of the Dead Sea Scrolls, had long characterized the Temple cult and its priests as wicked and false to the teachings of the Torah and the prophets. They had said the Temple itself was unclean, its worship defiled by associations with pagans. Links between the early Christian movement, the Qumran community, and Masada, the last stronghold of the Zealots against the Roman legions, are well documented. The community at Qumran reflected in the Dead Sea Scrolls was radically anti-Roman, antiestablishment, apocalyptic, and messianist, expectant of the restoration of the Davidic line to the throne of Israel; in the War Scroll found in one of their jars, this Davidic Messiah is called "the Scepter." They denounced the elite class of Sadducees, who controlled the corrupted worship in the Temple and exploited the poor with their demand for sacrifices and tithes. The Qumran sectarians believed themselves to be the pure remnant of Israel. Its members practiced rites similar to the later baptism of the early Christian community, and they marked the foreheads of their initiates with the sign given in Ezekiel 9 for marking the truly enlightened—those who grieved over the abominations practiced in Jerusalem. (Later Christian use of the X was believed to be the first initial of the Greek word *Christos*, but the actual practice of marking the initiated "elect" was the same!)[10]

The community at Qumran held itself aloof from those who collaborated with the Romans. Many of their beliefs and doctrines, hidden in jars for nearly two thousand years, echo the radical dualism and apocalypticism of the New Testament writings. Copies of some of the same manuscripts were also found at the fortress of Masada, the Zealot stronghold that fell to the Romans in A.D. 73 after the mass suicide of its defenders. Only in the last several decades, since their discovery in 1947, have biblical scholars had access to this invaluable information on the roots of the Christian movement. The partisans at Qumran would undoubtedly have applauded Jesus' radical overturning of the money tables in the Temple during the Passover feast.

Jesus of Nazareth, King of the Jews

Based on texts found in the canonical Greek Scriptures of the New Testament, there is good reason to believe that many Jews accepted Jesus as the promised Messiah of the line of David. The earliest written attestation to the fact that Jesus was believed by the Christian community to be the Davidic Messiah is found in Paul's Epistle to the Romans 1:3, thought to have been written about A.D. 57. It says of Jesus: ". . . who, as to his human nature was a descendant of David . . ." The Gospel of Mark (A.D. 71–75) records the triumphal entry of Jesus into Jerusalem, when the people spread palm fronds (John 12:13) before the king riding on a donkey. The palm tree is a symbol for the Jewish nation that is found on coins minted in Roman times. The fact that Jesus was believed to be king of the Jews is also affirmed by the inscription that Pilate ordered posted above the cross on which the Roman soldiers crucified him: "Jesus of Nazareth, King of the Jews," abbreviated "INRI." Galilee, the reputed homeland of Jesus, is now acknowledged to have been a hotbed of Zealot and anti-Roman activity during the first century A.D., which may be relevant to the ultimate charge of sedition.

There is ample evidence that Jesus was not just a poor carpenter or the son of a carpenter from an obscure town in Galilee. The evangelists Matthew and Luke, who were both writing at approximately the same time (between the years A.D. 80 and 85) but who were unaware of one another's work, include genealogies of Jesus at the beginning of their Gospels. Although these genealogies are at variance with one another, one thing can be inferred: the claim was being made that Jesus was the expected Davidic Messiah. The testimony of both of these Gospels is that the Roman governor and the Jewish leaders collaborated in the arrest and crucifixion of Jesus because he was perceived by both Jewish and Roman authorities to be a dangerous insurrectionist. His death was believed by these authorities to be a political necessity in order to avoid further rebellion in Palestine. He was considered incendiary because the people believed he was their promised Messiah and king, the Anointed One of God, the "just ruler" proclaimed by their prophets. From the Gospels, we surmise that Jesus was the people's choice because his miracles proved to them that he was Yahweh's choice.

The power of the people is often feared by a repressive establishment because it threatens the stability of the status quo. According to the Gospels, written with an eye toward converting citizens of the Roman Empire to the Christian way, it was the will of the *Jewish* authorities that Jesus be crucified. *But crucifixion was not a Jewish punishment.* If the charge against Jesus had been blasphemy, as is suggested in the Gospels, Jesus would have been stoned by the Jewish community (as was his disciple Stephen in Acts 7), not crucified. *Crucifixion was a Roman execution reserved specifically for seditionists.* It seems to have been the public acclaim of Jesus as king that led to his execution as an enemy of Rome.

The Gospels record that Jesus was not only a political figure, the King of the Jews, but that he was also a religious leader who called to the people to repent and prepare for the Kingdom of God. He repeatedly challenged the religious leaders concerning their teachings and their interpretation of Scripture. And he was a healer. In a book entitled *Jesus the Magician*, ancient Middle Eastern sources are quoted in an attempt to show that Jesus was one of the traveling wonderworkers of the time.[11] However, it seems far more likely from the scriptural accounts that Jesus was a genuinely charismatic healer who understood the psychic phenomenon of people being healed as a dynamic of their own faith. In fact, Jesus often says exactly that: "Your faith has made you whole!"

According to Luke's Gospel, Jesus visited the synagogue in Nazareth and read aloud to the congregation from the prophecy of Isaiah (61:1–2):

> The Spirit of God is upon me,
> because the Lord has anointed me.
> He has sent me to bring
> glad tidings to the lowly,
> to heal the brokenhearted,
> to proclaim liberty to the captive
> and release to the prisoners.

It has been the consensus of Christians for nearly two thousand years that the man who appropriated these verses to himself was no mere magician. He was an earthen vessel filled with the Spirit of God. And it was this powerful charisma that so inevitably led to his crucifixion as a political incendiary and to the desperate flight of his immediate family from Jerusalem.

The Flowering Staff and the Sangraal

What does legend say about the refugee Holy Family? Scripture, of course, in the New Testament Gospel of Matthew, reports that a "Holy Family" fled to Egypt to avoid having its child murdered by King Herod, who was worried about his claim to the throne of Israel. Joseph, "the husband of Mary," was told in a dream to take Mary and Jesus and flee into Egypt (Matt. 2:13). The widely held belief of many modern biblical scholars is that this is "mythology," used by the author of Matthew's gospel to fulfill the word of the Prophet: "out of Egypt I called my son" (Hos. 11:1b). The "fossil of truth" in this story is the strong tradition of danger to the royal bloodline of Judah. An apocryphal gospel is the source of the tradition that Saint Joseph's staff sprouted as a sign from God that he was chosen to be the husband of Mary and the earthly father of her child. But the "flowering staff," which is shown in Saint Joseph's hand in Catholic churches worldwide, also serves to remind us that Joseph was the custodian of the "shoot," understood to be Jesus himself based on the prophecy of Isaiah: "A shoot shall sprout from the stump of Jesse, and from his root a bud shall blossom" (Isaiah 11:1).

But tradition derived from an Old French legend from the Mediterranean coast tells us that another Joseph, Joseph of Arimathea, was the custodian of the "Sangraal" and that the child on the boat was Egyptian, which means quite literally "born in Egypt." It seems likely that after the crucifixion of Jesus, Mary the Magdalen found it necessary to flee for the sake of her unborn child to the nearest refuge. The influential friend of Jesus, Joseph of Arimathea, could very well have been her protector.

If our theory is correct, the child actually *was* born in Egypt. Egypt was the traditional place of asylum for Jews whose safety was threatened in Israel; Alexandria was easily reached from Judea and contained well-established Jewish communities at the time of Jesus.[12] In all probability, the emergency refuge of Mary Magdalen and Joseph of Arimathea was Egypt. And later—years later—they left Alexandria and sought an even safer haven on the coast of France.

Scholars of archaeology and linguistics have found that place names and legends of an area contain "fossils" from that area's remote past. The truth may be embellished by changes and stories may suffer abridgment through the years of telling, but traces of the truth remain in fossil form, buried in the names of people and places. In the town of Les Saintes-Maries-de-la-Mer in France, there is a festival every May 23 to 25 at a shrine in honor of Saint Sarah the Egyptian, also called Sara Kali, the "Black Queen." Close scrutiny reveals that this festival, which originated in the Middle Ages, is in honor of an "Egyptian" child who accompanied Mary Magdalen, Martha, and Lazarus, arriving with them in a small boat that came ashore at this location in approximately A.D. 42. The people seem to have assumed that the child, being "Egyptian," was dark-skinned and, by further interpolation, that she must have been the servant of the family from Bethany, since no other reasonable explanation could be found for her presence.

The name Sarah means "queen" or "princess" in Hebrew. This Sarah is further characterized in local legends as "young," no more than a child. So we have, in a tiny coastal town in France, a yearly festival in honor of a young, dark-skinned girl-child called Sarah. The fossil in this legend is that the child is called "princess" in Hebrew. A child of Jesus, born after Mary's flight to Alexandria, would have been about twelve years of age at the time of the voyage to Gaul recorded in the legend. She, like the princes of David's line, is *symbolically* black, "unrecognized in the streets" (Lam. 4:8). The Magdalen was herself the "Sangraal," in the sense that she was the "chalice" or vessel that once carried the royal bloodline *in utero*. The symbolic blackness of the Bride in Canticles and the Davidic princes of Lamentations is extended to this hidden Mary and her child. It appears that the festival of the Black Princess, Sara Kali, is in honor of this same symbolically black child. (In a later chapter we will investigate more closely the shrines of the Black Madonna in Western Europe.)

It is likely that those in later centuries who knew this legend and the identity of the Magdalen as the wife of Jesus equated her with the black bride from Canticles. She was the Sister-Bride and the Beloved. Her "blackness" would have been symbolic of her hidden state; she was the unknown queen—unacknowledged, repudiated, and vilified by the church through the centuries in an attempt to deny the legitimate bloodline and to maintain its own doctrines of the divinity and celibacy of Jesus. Her blackness is also a direct reference to the deposed Davidic princes of Jerusalem: "Brighter than snow were her princes, whiter than milk . . . now their appearance is blacker than soot, they are unrecognized on the streets" (Lam. 4:8).

Fossils of truth remain buried in our symbols, our proper names of persons and places, our rituals and folk tales. This understood, it is plausible that the flight into Egypt was taken by the "other Joseph," Joseph of Arimathea, and the "other Mary," Mary Magdalen, to protect the unborn child of Jesus from the Romans and the sons of Herod after the crucifixion. The discrepancies in the story and the obvious generation gap can easily be understood in light of the danger to the bloodline—which required the utmost secrecy as to their whereabouts—and in light of the time that elapsed before the story was committed to writing. This seems to be another case of a myth being formed because the truth was too dangerous to be told.

The Merovingian Connection

There is evidence to suggest that the royal bloodline of Jesus and Mary Magdalen eventually flowed in the veins of the Merovingian monarchs of France. The name *Merovingian* may itself be a linguistic fossil. The lore surrounding the royal family of the Franks mentions an ancestor "Merovée." But the word *Merovingian* breaks down phonetically into syllables that we can easily recognize: *mer* and *vin*, Mary and the vine. Broken down this way, it may be seen to allude to the "vine of Mary" or perhaps the "vine of the Mother."

The royal emblem of the Merovingian King Clovis was the fleur-de-lis (the iris). The Latin name for the iris flower, which grows wild in countries of the Middle East, is *gladiolus*, or "small sword." The trefoil fleur-de-lis of the royal house of France is a masculine symbol. In fact, it is a graphic image of the covenant of circumcision in which are inherent all the promises of God to Israel and to the House of David. Thomas Inman discusses the masculine nature of the "flower of light" at length in his nineteenth-century work *Ancient Pagan and Modern Christian Symbolism*. It is almost amusing that this same male symbol, the "little sword," is today the international emblem for the Boy Scouts!

The assertion that this symbol represents the Trinity is a rationalization based on its three-in-one image. This three-pronged "lily" is an ancient symbol for Israel: the capitals of the two phallic pillars of Solomon's Temple, Jachin and Boaz, were carved with "lilywork"

(1 Kings 7:22). The famed shamrock of Saint Patrick may be a legitimate symbol for the Trinity, but I believe that the fleur-de-lis refers specifically to the Davidic bloodline of Israel and was used as their emblem by the royal Merovingians in Europe.

The grave of the Merovingian King Childeric I (who died circa A.D. 481) was discovered in 1653 in Tournai and was found to contain three hundred golden bees. The bee was known to have been the family totem of the Merovingian kings. Bees were sacred symbols of the goddess of love and were also an Egyptian symbol for royalty. Bee colonies are matriarchal, recognizing the queen as their monarch. I think it likely that the totem of the golden bee was consciously chosen to reflect the descent of the Merovingian line from the royal house of David (and hence Jesus) through the female line and that they honored the royal widow, Mary Magdalen, and her daughter, whom legend calls Sarah.

The royal bloodline of Israel may have survived persecution and eventually surfaced in the Merovingians of Europe and in related families that guarded their secret genealogies through the centuries. The First Crusade (A.D. 1098) could then conceivably have been an attempt to restore an heir of the Davidic bloodline to the throne of Jerusalem in the person of Godfroi of Bouillon (also known as Godfroi of Lorraine), who was, according to legend, of Merovingian lineage.[13]

With the conquest of Jerusalem in 1099, the leaders of the Crusade installed a patriarch in the Church of the Holy Sepulchre in Jerusalem. And in their liturgical formulae we find the bizarre fact that all feasts of the Virgin Mary were to be marked by *black* vestments.[14] It is suggested that this use had reference to the Song of Songs, but it was a marked departure from the universal custom of the church in which white vestments were worn for all liturgies on Marian feast days.[15] Perhaps the black vestments are again a symbolic reference to the *other* Mary, the hidden one, the Lost Bride from the Canticles, scorned and repudiated by the orthodox church—the exiled queen whose true identity had been secretly guarded for centuries, first from the Roman authorities and Herod's heirs and then from the hierarchy of the Roman Catholic Church. This "black" Mary would be a poetic echo of the dark Bride from the Song of Songs, the Bride of the sacrificed Shepherd-King, the messianic Bridegroom of Israel.

These associations of the Black Bride may be the reason for the immense popularity of the numerous shrines to the Black Madonna scattered throughout Western Europe. The image of the Sister-Bride from the ancient world was easily associated with the wife of Jesus Christ, the Anointed One. Classical replicas of the Earth, moon, and love goddesses (Isis, Artemis of Ephesus, and others) were characteristically black.

In summary, the two royal refugees from Israel, mother and daughter, might logically be represented in early European art as a dark-skinned mother and child, the hidden ones. The Black Madonnas of the early shrines in Europe (fifth to twelfth centuries) might then have been venerated as symbolic of this other Mary and her child, the Sangraal, which Joseph of Arimathea brought in safety to the coast of France. The symbol for a male of the royal house of David would be a flowering or budding staff, but the symbol for a woman would be the chalice—a cup or vessel containing the royal blood of Jesus. And that is exactly what the Holy Grail is said to have been!

THE TWELFTH-CENTURY AWAKENING

This version of the Christian story we are examining is not taught in established Christian churches, yet it may be closer to the truth than the "orthodox" version. In fact, there were numerous early versions of Christianity that did not survive. For example, the Church of Jerusalem, of which Jesus' brother James was the first leader, remained very Jewish in orientation and did not equate Jesus with God. The Christian community in Jerusalem remained loyal to the Temple and the Torah of Judaism. James and Peter, the two preeminent leaders of the Jerusalem community, were demonstrably disturbed by the version of Christianity taught by Paul. In Paul's Epistles and in the Book of Acts we find evidence that these two Apostles repudiated some of Paul's teachings. The followers of Paul's version of Christianity eventually began to speak scornfully of the family of Jesus and of the original band of Apostles, who they felt had not fully understood Jesus. This position is suggested in Mark's Gospel, where the family and friends of Jesus consider him to have gone mad (Mark 3:21). The Gospel writers also state that Jesus chided the Apostles for being obtuse. Peter especially is singled out for having misunderstood the necessity for the crucifixion and for having denied Jesus three times on the night of his arrest.

Many Christologies developed in the early church; heated struggles between factions continued for centuries. With the disbanding of the Christian community in Jerusalem following the Jewish Revolt in A.D. 66–74, there was no authoritative version of Christianity that could claim to be the only authentic faith. Eventually some sects were driven out of the church, while others compromised. The Ebionites, close spiritual descendants of the early Jerusalem community of James and Peter, were later branded heretical because their "low" Christology did not attribute divinity to the historical Jesus of Nazareth.

The records and teachings of the deviant sects and factions have not survived the centuries. In many cases, the only mention of heretical teachings is found in the polemic of one or another of the church fathers who wished to expose their error. The first four centuries of the church were marked with turmoil, persecution, and heterodox interpretations. The Council of Nicaea (A.D. 325) proclaimed that Jesus was the "only begotten Son of the Father, Light from Light, true God from true God, of one being with the Father." This became the orthodox creed of the empire, and no variations were tolerated. Missionaries of this creed set out to convert heathen tribes in remote corners of Europe, preaching the Gospel as mandated by their Lord Jesus and baptizing in the name of their Trinity: the Father, the Son, and the Holy Spirit. Following the edict by Emperor Theodosius that declared Christianity the official religion of the Roman Empire in A.D. 380, versions of Christianity that did not agree with that of the newly empowered hierarchy of bishops were ruthlessly persecuted and their teachings destroyed.

The Dark Ages

The general pillage and turmoil of the period between the fourth and the tenth centuries in Europe, wrought by the sweep of the barbarian tribes—Frank, Visigoth, Celt, Hun, and eventually Norse—led to a relative dearth of written records of the era. There is also some evidence that the records that did exist were deliberately expunged during the period we now call the Dark Ages.

Most of the Western European barbarian tribes were originally converted to the Arian heresy, a form of Christianity articulated by a fourth-century native of Alexandria who found himself vehemently condemned at the Council of Nicaea. The Arian heresy denied the doctrines of the Holy Trinity and the divinity of Jesus, instead preaching the existence of an all-powerful God and his son, a fully human Jesus. This version of Christianity was widespread in Western Europe during the fifth and sixth centuries.

The history of the Dark Ages has been painstakingly reconstructed with the aid of documents found in monasteries and cloisters and through numerous finds by archaeologists. By these means, the tragic history of the obscured Merovingian kings has been brought to light: Childeric III, the last of the legitimate Merovingian kings, was deposed in A.D. 751 by Pepin, the royal steward whose descendants through his grandson Charlemagne became known as the Carolingians. The title Holy Roman Emperor was conferred on Charlemagne by the pope on Christmas Day, A.D. 800. During his reign, Charlemagne encouraged arts and letters, including the copying and preserving of manuscripts. Those who lived in this period did not call it "dark."

The great European centers of civilization during this era were Celtic Ireland, Moorish Spain, and the Mediterranean coast of what is now France. We are most concerned with the latter, since it was the seedbed of the legends and the heresy of the Sangraal. This region was known interchangeably as Occitania, the Languedoc, or the Midi. Today it is most commonly called Provence.

The Cradle of the Awakening

A number of students of European history are agreed that the first real awakening from the Dark Ages in Europe was not the fifteenth-century Renaissance, as is usually assumed, but rather certain events that occurred in southern France in the twelfth century. Tomes have been written on the influence of the Crusades, the cross-fertilization of ideas of the East and West, the impact of Moslem art and thought on this region, and the rise of craftspeople and the middle-class bourgeoisie. But Provence had been an area of relative enlightenment and progress for centuries prior to the Crusades, pursuing a lively interest in Islamic and Jewish religion, arts, and literature, and tolerating new ideas in science and philosophy. This openness to diversity fostered in the Midi a sophistication unmatched in the northern countries of continental Europe.

Perhaps the most important of all the many profound social changes in twelfth-century Europe was a growing appreciation of the feminine. This radical shift was rooted in Provence, where practices were at striking variance with the rest of the medieval world. Basically the medieval attitude at this time was misogynistic. Hostility toward women was founded on the stated position of the church fathers, which was in part based on the story of Adam and Eve in the garden of Eden (Genesis 1, 2). The writings of the Christian patriarchs, most notably those of the fifth-century saints Augustine of Hippo (354–430) and Jerome (342–420), viewed women as morally and spiritually inferior to men. Later theologians even debated whether or not a woman could be said to have a soul. Women, sex, and the human body, along with all earthly pleasures, were officially regarded as distractions and temptations that could lure men away from the spiritual path.

The beliefs regarding women held by most of the Christian world in medieval times were radically dualistic. The material world, the flesh, the devil, and women were lumped together as a source of evil that kept men from attaining spiritual union with God. In order to free the soul for spiritual pursuits, these evils had to be denied and overcome. Desires of the flesh were to be scorned and ignored if possible.

The views of Saint Augustine had enormous influence on the attitudes toward women and sex, and they seem to reflect the influence of the Manichaean heresy, named for its founder, Mani, who died in A.D. 277. Augustine was an adherent of this heresy until his conversion to Christianity at the age of thirty-one, after a youth of debauchery. Mani had taught that the god of the Old Testament was a demigod who created the world and all its evils, entrapping pure spirits in the "prison" of human flesh. Women, quite logically, were considered prime agents of the perpetuation of the miseries of the physical world, and conception of children was necessarily discouraged by the followers of Mani. Augustine went on after his conversion to become the preeminent interpreter of Catholic doctrine and scripture, bringing with him remnants of his former dualistic worldview and basic misogyny.

In medieval Europe, women had no legal rights and were the wards of their fathers or husbands. They were excluded from the civic life of their society and owned no property. They were mere chattels. The only significant exception to this was the attitude toward women among the people of Southern France. There, along with men, women held many fiefs and manors by right of inheritance as early as the tenth century. The reasons for this may have been the people's strong ties to egalitarian Roman practices or to even more ancient tribal traditions.

But I suspect that there was an even more obvious reason. Since the dawn of Christianity, this area had a very strong history of honoring women. During the eleventh and twelfth centuries, the women of Provence were held in especially high regard. A classic example of the "liberated woman" in the medieval world was Eleanor of Aquitaine (1122–1204), whose notoriety and power plays as wife and mother of kings shook Europe for decades.

The Crusades are often cited as the catalyst for the reawakening of culture in Europe after the long period dubbed the Dark Ages. But Provence had maintained an enlightened relationship with the Moorish and Jewish centers of learning in Spain and North Africa for several hundred years prior to the Crusades, and its flourishing culture had been influenced by this openness. In fact, much of the area of Provence had been included in the eighth-century Jewish kingdom of Septimania under Guillem of Gellone, a Jewish Prince of Merovingian descent.[1] And this same area had been the center of a cult of Mary Magdalen for centuries, as witness the numerous chapels, fountains, springs, and other geographical landmarks in the region that bear her name. She was the patron saint of gardens and vineyards throughout the region, the mediatrix of fertility, beauty, and the joy of life. Hers were the ancient domains of the love goddesses of antiquity. It was not accidental that the cult of the Rose (an anagram of *Eros*) flourished and bloomed in the garden of Provence.

When Peter the Hermit, the monk who instigated the First Crusade, preached in Europe's towns during the final decade of the eleventh century, he argued that it was time for a "holy war" to win Jerusalem back from the Saracens. He was, figuratively speaking, carrying an hourglass. One millennium had passed since the destruction of the Temple of Jerusalem by the Romans, who burned it to the ground in A.D. 70 and laid the city waste. Peter proclaimed to the towns of Europe that it was time to restore the Holy City and rebuild the Temple. The secret agenda of Peter the Hermit and his influential friends was to put a descendant of David's line on the throne of Jerusalem,[2] thus "assisting God" in bringing about the prophesied millennium of peace and promise outlined in the Hebrew Scriptures.

All the knights of Europe who could bear arms embarked for the Holy Land, some on foot, others in ships. In the year 1099, their dream at last was realized: the Saracens were defeated, and Godfroi of Lorraine, a nobleman allegedly of Merovingian lineage,[3] was offered the title Baron of Jerusalem. The group who had orchestrated this agenda seemed satisfied with the results of their political coup. With a scion of David finally restored to Jerusalem, numerous stories, poems, and songs—and eventually the Grail legends themselves—began to bloom in abundance. Throughout Christendom, an emerging culture extolled the popular hero Godfroi, the Crusaders, and "Our Lady." The seeds of this culture, originally carried to western Europe by Mary Magdalen, had germinated in the fertile soil of Provence.

One of the intriguing footnotes from the period of the early Crusades is the story of the rapid rise and eclipse of the vastly powerful chivalric Order of the Knights Templar. This order of warrior-clerics was officially formed in the first decades of the twelfth century following the recapture of Jerusalem, and it enjoyed the favor of popes and kings for almost two centuries before its annihilation on charges of heresy in the opening decade of the fourteenth century. The authors of *The Holy Blood and the Holy Grail* researched the origins and history of the Order of the Knights Templar exhaustively. They concluded that it was closely involved with the heretical sects of Christianity that believed that Jesus was fully human and married, that his royal blood still flowed in the veins of the noble families of Provence, and that the messianic promises of the Hebrew Scriptures would someday be fulfilled in a descendant of Jesus. Many of the Knights Templar sprang from noble families in Provence, an area that had always held itself aloof from the official doctrines of Rome.

The Heretics of Provence

The "alternative Gospel"—the Arian heresy and the later heresies of the Cathars and Waldensians—flourished through the first twelve centuries of Christianity in this region. Although the tenets of the heresies differed, one thing is clear: Provence never wholeheartedly accepted the orthodox version of Roman Catholicism and its creed. It had its reasons.

The term *Albigensian* was coined in A.D. 1165 after a church council met in the town of Albi to issue an edict condemning the heretics of the Midi—in particular the sect called the Cathars. Based on this edict of Albi, the heretics of the entire region are often indiscriminately called Albigensians, regardless of the tenets of the particular heresy to which they adhered. The people of this area had proved themselves tolerant of both Jewish and Moorish cultures, willing to share in their philosophical and esoteric traditions and to criticize the hierarchy of the Roman Church, many of whose clerics, it is widely admitted, were guilty of corruption and abuses during the eleventh and twelfth centuries. Often there seems to have been a chasm between their preaching and their practice of the Gospel. The whole northern coast washed by the Mediterranean was in ferment with the cross-pollinating stimuli of the era, and freedom was the rallying cry. The families of the Provence were no allies of the king of France, nor did they wish to be Rome's minions. Their distinguishing feature was independence.

The Faith of the Cathars

The citizens of the region, among whom the Cathar heresy had an ever stronger hold in the twelfth century, were simple farmers and peasants. They heard the sermons of the itinerant preachers, the Cathari, called the "pure ones," who came and worked in their fields, shared their bread, and preached to them, urging them to live their lives in the simplicity and humble spirit of Jesus. Known as "credants," they believed their version of Christianity to be both purer and older than orthodox Christianity, closer to the teachings of Jesus and the Apostles than the orthodox version of the faith. They were often vegetarian and pacifist, practicing a mode of charismatic Christianity similar to that of the early church described in the Book of Acts in the New Testament. The few remaining documents that survived the censorship of the Inquisition verify that the Cathars' practice of Christianity had roots both ancient and pure, reflecting the vigor of primitive Christianity at its dawn.[4]

The charges of Manichaeanism and radical dualism leveled by the Inquisition against this sect were most likely exaggerated. There is no mention of Mani in any surviving Cathar document. It seems more probable that the ancient roots of Catharism are to be found in first-century Christian practice and that they sprang from the same apocalyptic dualism as did the earliest Judeo-Christian sects and the desert community at Qumran. The Cathars' interest in the spiritual life and their lack of enthusiasm for the institution of marriage— because it condemned the spirit to a fleshly existence—echo strongly the beliefs of the apocalyptic Judeo-Christian communities of the first century. Saint Paul and the earliest adherents of the Christian way believed that the end of the age was so imminent that there was really no point in getting married. A list of the noble families who openly adhered to the Cathar faith survived, and this list refutes the charge of the inquisitors that the members of the heretical church tried to undermine the institution of family by condemning marriage or the conception of children. It is likely that they refused to be wed in orthodox wedding ceremonies, but that may have been on the grounds that they did not consider those ceremonies valid or necessary. For the same reasons, they also refused the baptism of the Roman Church.

The Cathari preached a lifestyle of simple living and radical faith in God's continual presence and guidance. One did not have to have ties to Manichaeanism to believe that the devil was "Prince of this world." Jesus is quoted as having been of that opinion himself (John 12:31)! The Cathars may not have been Manichaean so much as close adherents to the literal texts of the Gospels, of which each Cathar family owned a copy. For these Albigensian heretics, the faith was not a doctrine to be believed but a life to be lived. They called themselves Christians.

Fundamental to the teachings of the "Church of Love," another name for the alternative church, was a profound devotion to Jesus, the Light Bearer, and to his mother and friends. While the church in Rome taught obedience to rules and strict practice of its laws and prohibitions, the Church of "Amor" ("Roma" spelled backward!) taught that each individual life must be transformed into holiness by the action of the Holy Spirit in mind and heart. The adherents to the alternative church honored Jesus as their prophet, priest, king, and Messiah—a fully human agent and the anointed Son of God. But they understood their own role as earthen vessels of that same Holy Spirit. They were aware of the mythological and mystical content of Christ's teachings as a path to holiness and transformation, and they were aware of its connections with the entire stream of revelation and religious consciousness of the classical world. They did not consider the exoteric practices of dowsing in a baptismal font or attendance at Sunday Mass sufficient for salvation; their religion was a practice of the presence of God and daily growth in the virtues of charity, humility, and service to others modeled on the life and teachings of Jesus himself.

In the Midi, antagonism toward the Catholic Church was both

deep and wide. It was the experience of the people of Provence, and indeed in many other places, that the hierarchy of the institutional church did not live the Gospel message. Clerics often exploited the poor and lived in comparative luxury while their parishioners starved. The Albigensian sects were distinctly anticlerical and antiecclesiastic. The Cathars formed their own church in opposition to what they believed was the false teaching of Rome. They repudiated the ritual of the Mass and the cross because it was the instrument of torture, in no way worthy of veneration. They claimed that their own church had retained the Holy Spirit conferred on the original Apostles at Pentecost and passed on by the laying on of hands, the only ritual that they regarded as authentic. The fundamental and oft-recited prayer of this alternative church was the "Our Father" found in Matthew's Gospel. The Catharist ritual, of which two texts have survived, demonstrates that they possessed ancient documents directly inspired by the primitive Christian community.[5]

The faith of the Cathars did not need a cultic priesthood or a church building containing artifacts and relics. Their faith was practiced in their homes and fields. They disdained the need for churches, relics, and sacramentals. Among the Cathars, men and women were considered equals, women even being allowed to inherit and own property, as we have noted. Women were also allowed to preach, a practice that had begun in the early Christian community but that had long since been discontinued in Roman Catholicism. This practice among the Cathars reflected the esteem in which the women, including Mary Magdalen, had once been held in the infant church. Cathar preachers, both men and women, traveled though the countryside in pairs, just as the early disciples of Jesus had done in Palestine, sharing the fare of the poor, working side by side with them in the fields, and preaching the simple and pure life of the spiritually enlightened. Saint Dominic and later Saint Francis of Assisi were so impressed with the Cathar methods of evangelizing converts that they modeled their mendicant friars along these same lines, taking vows of poverty and charity.

One extraordinary feature of the Cathars was their insistence that the Bible be translated into their language, the regional *langue d'oc* dialect, and the people taught to read the Good News of Jesus in their own tongue. To this end, numerous paper mills sprang up all over the region, giving impetus to the resurgence of art, thought, and letters throughout Provence and later the whole of Europe. Cathar children were taught to read, the girls often becoming better educated than their male counterparts. Provence was an enlightened domain.

In 1209 the Vatican launched a crusade against the entire region of Provence, including the nobility of the area, many of whom had themselves embraced the Cathar heresy. Allied with the king of France, the armies of the pope ravaged the Midi for a generation, their victory culminating in the massacre of Montségur, a Cathar seminary. There, in 1244, an enclave of besieged heretics was defeated, and more than two hundred who refused to recant were burned at the stake. The backbone of what was known as "Catharism" was broken by the Albigensian Crusade, as this frightful episode is called, and the flowering begun in the twelfth century was nipped in the bud.

The Inquisition, formally instituted in 1233, ruthlessly interrogated and sentenced heretics, executing thousands. The records of the Inquisition are not always clear as to what heretical beliefs the church fathers in Rome found so offensive. In fact, most of the documents of the Albigensian heresy were destroyed. Naturally it was not in the interests of the Vatican and its strong right arm, the Inquisition, to retain documents that might promulgate the very doctrines they were trying desperately to expunge.

In examining the Albigensian Crusade from our vantage point, it seems clear that it was an attempt to force an entire region into the orthodoxy of Rome and to destroy the families who resisted. Since the deviant thought, culture, and underlying beliefs of Provence were found to be at odds with the orthodox version of the faith, every attempt was made to blot them from memory. The truth is that the entire region was opposed, for numerous reasons and in numerous ways, to the hegemony of the Roman Church.

We have already discussed one fundamental aspect of this deep-rooted disenchantment with the established church. The belief that Jesus was married and had heirs was indigenous to Provence. Mary Magdalen was believed to have lived on their soil and to have been buried there, along with her brother, her sister, and several close friends. The legends and place names of Provence confirmed these beliefs. And so did the secret genealogies of their noble families.[6] Following the Albigensian Crusade, surviving daughters of the noble families of the Midi were forced to marry into families in the north, presumably to dissipate the exclusive claims of certain southern families to their special Merovingian bloodline. That was not new. In fact, to consolidate his claim to the throne of the Franks, Charlemagne's father had himself married a Merovingian princess.

The flowering of the feminine principle in Provence had one very specific cause that has been overlooked by historians who suggest that the Crusaders brought back the new cultural trends from the Middle East: the adherents of the hidden "Church of the Grail" believed that it was time to claim their heritage and make known their version of the Christian faith. The king of Jerusalem was a scion of David. The Davidic "anointed" had been offered the throne of his fathers in the person of Godfroi of Lorraine in the year 1099.

Following the naming of Godfroi's heirs to the title King of Jerusalem, poets became freer with the stories and legends of the Sangraal, and a large number of Grail romances blossomed. The poets residing in the courts of the nobility of Europe were free at last to spin their yarns, broadly hinting at the prestige and role of the Grail Family. The stories of Parsifal's search for the Grail were told in every court, and the legends of King Arthur, first written by the ninth-century Welsh cleric Nennius, were linked to the Grail and began to grow in all sorts of directions—always with the search for the Grail as the underlying motif. The list of the twelfth-century court poets who wrote these early Grail epics includes Guiot de Provins, Robert de Boron, Chrétien de Troyes, Walter Map, and Wolfram von Eschenbach.

It is occasionally suggested that the earliest version of the Grail story was known to the Moors in Spain and later brought to France. But the original "Sangraal" of the Old French legends is a distinctly Christian myth and is much older than the Moorish presence in Spain, much older even than the faith of Islam. It is indigenous to Provence. In fact, as we have seen, the earliest legends indicate that the Sangraal was brought ashore in A.D. 42 at Les Saintes-Maries-de-la-Mer. It may later have become associated with the ancient Celtic legends of the magical Cauldron of Bran, also native to Europe, but that Celtic vessel is not called the Sangraal. The word *Sangraal* is reserved very specifically to the chalice or "vessel" that once contained the blood of Christ.

The Troubadours

An interesting aside to the Albigensian Crusade against the sectarians of Provence is the fate of the troubadours. These twelfth- and thirteenth-century singers and songwriters extolled the virtues of their "Lady"—a woman who was in every way beautiful and lovable, whose servant they desired to be in all things, whose favor they wished to win, and whose praises they could not resist singing. She was often called "Dompna" in their songs, which is the *lange d'oc* word for the Latin *Domina*, the feminine of *Dominus*, or "Lord." (The most common of all the titles given to Jesus in the Latin liturgies of the Catholic Church is Dominus.)

The Dompna of the troubadours was the source of their life's joy and enthusiasm, their motive for taking the Crusaders' cross and for restoring the Holy Land to Christianity. She was their mentor and patroness. Often the Lady was a secret love, although they sang her praises aloud! And the things they knew about her were held in confidence, along with her name. She was simply "Lady." The troubadour was her humble and obedient vassal, sworn to secrecy and fidelity. His only remuneration was to become ennobled by his association with his Lady.

Examples of this sentiment in the poems of the troubadours are frequent, as in these lines from a song by the twelfth-century poet Arnaut Daniel:

> Each day I am a better man and purer
> for I serve the noblest lady in the world,
> and I worship her, I tell you this in the open.[7]

So often were sentiments expressed honoring Dompna that more than one scholar has suggested that perhaps they were all singing the praises of the same Lady, or perhaps an ideal "feminine," rather than a particular lady (although clearly many of the troubadours' poems *were* addressed to a specific human mentor or lover).

Modern scholars who have studied the genre of courtly love songs of the troubadours of Provence have occasionally suggested that the poets were secretly Cathars and that this Lady was the cult or heresy itself, the Church of Amor that gave them secret solace and inspired their poetry.[8] The work of Denis de Rougemont in particular is cited as suggesting that the troubadours were Cathars. One troubadour, Peire Vidal, is mentioned as praising and thanking certain courts in Provence for their gracious hospitality. Every court the poet mentions is known to have been a "mother house" of the Cathar heresy.[9]

It is true that the troubadours were interrogated by special papal legates and later by the Inquisition, which was created for the express purpose of identifying heretics in Provence. True to this intention, the minstrels and their poetry were found to be heretical. In 1209 the troubadour Gui D'Ussel was told by a papal legate to cease composing.[10] Many troubadours went into exile, while others changed their songs. And eventually the Lady became idealized and immortal, an "eternal feminine principle" or often the *Virgin* "Saint Mary." But the original Saint Mary of the courtly poets—their Dompna—was, I believe, the patron saint of their region, where chapels to the Magdalen are inevitable and frequent, and where her cult flourished from the end of the eighth century.[11] She was their Domina, the feminine counterpart of Dominus, the Lord—not prostitute, but Lady.

The Rising Cult of the Virgin Mother

The flowering of civilization in the twelfth century under the gentle tutelage of "Our Lady" encouraged the pursuit of astronomy and mathematics, medicine and mysticism, art and architecture. These disciplines, which included the ancient practice of sacred geometry, were greatly enhanced by contact with the highly developed civilization of Islam. For this brief 120 years, from the return of the veterans of the First Crusade until the Inquisition moved to stifle it, medieval civilization bloomed profusely.

Perceiving danger in allowing the rumor of Jesus' marriage and alleged bloodline to circulate, the Church of Rome moved quickly and firmly in the thirteenth century to ensure that it was the mother of Jesus, not his wife, who was venerated by the faithful. All Christians honored the mother of Jesus and found solace in her advocacy. Preeminent among her many shrines was the Cathedral of Chartres, which was the site of an ancient cult to the Black Madonna, centered around a statue known as "Our Lady under the Earth," located in a grotto under the structure.

Pilgrims have sought Our Lady's shrine at Chartres since pre-Christian times. Today they continue to flock to the healing waters of the "Well of the Strong" in the crypt where the original statue of the Madonna was enthroned. This Madonna's statue was destroyed in the sixteenth century; however, legend holds that the shrine, sacred to the Mother Goddess so often worshiped at a well or spring, was deemed holy by Druids long before Christians adopted it. Sanctioned by the Church of Rome, the cult of Our Lady and of the feminine (including mysticism, healing, and transformation) flourished at the medieval school at Chartres, which became a noted center of enlightenment, the seat of a cult of "Maria-Sophia," goddess of wisdom.

The present cathedral, built between 1194 and 1220 over the sacred grotto containing the statue, is a Gothic monument to the doctrine of perfect balance and harmony. Louis Charpentier, a scholar-mystic who studied Chartres Cathedral in great depth, believes that the Order of the Knights of the Temple, or Knights Templar, were behind its design and construction as well as that of others built in France between 1130 and 1250.[12] The Order of the Knights of the Temple created an extensive network of building and farming enterprises that stimulated the economy in French towns, bringing a new prosperity to the region. As their name implies, their special work was the building of monasteries, churches, and cathedrals. I believe this vocation was at the leading edge of the attempt to restore the feminine principle to medieval society.

The Builders of the Temples

It had been suggested that the Order of the Knights of the Temple had access to the esoteric wisdom of the classical world, perhaps preserved in Islamic sources that members of the order encountered in the Middle East. Their knowledge of mathematics and engineering gave birth to the Gothic style of architecture, which spread almost overnight, as if by prior plan, across the face of Europe during the period from 1130 to 1250. The delicate balance of thrust and counterthrust, the harmony in stone of these cathedrals, many of which were dedicated to Our Lady, attest to a knowledge of geometry and an engineering technology far beyond any previously practiced in Europe.

There seems to be a strong connection between the Knights Templar and the development of the mason's craft and the guilds that built Europe's Gothic cathedrals. The Knights of the Temple planned and financed the temples, and guilds of stonemasons were formed to implement their designs. These masons are said to have built the tenets of their faith into the cathedrals, a faith that was expressed through the language of mathematics and symbol. Paramount among the tenets of this faith was the cosmic principle of the harmony of male and female energies.

Many of the secrets of the Templars may yet be discovered by examining the measurements and details of their edifices. The guild of masons who built Chartres and others of the French cathedrals of this period called themselves the Children of Solomon,[13] a clear reference to King David's son who built the first Jewish Temple of Jerusalem. But the name has even deeper associations. Solomon was also renowned for his wisdom, and it is he who is claimed to have written the Song of Songs, the love song of the *hieros gamos* of the ancient world. The Book of Wisdom also holds that Solomon sought Wisdom as his bride. So the name of the guild of masons who built the cathedrals serves to connect us with the wisdom tradition of ancient Judaism. And their vocation was the building of temples that would restore the feminine principle to the medieval world.

The Inquisition's ruthless campaign against the Albigensian heresy and the prominent families of Provence, many of whom were Templars, quickly squelched the budding of the feminine and its corollary branches of art and science. Louis Charpentier, in his book *The Mysteries of Chartres Cathedral*, notes that the spirit that had inspired the authentic Gothic cathedrals inexplicably departed after 1250, although flamboyant "virtuoso" copies of the style continued to be built.

Perhaps we can explain this enigmatic flight of the Spirit. The year 1250 corresponds to the rising power of the inquisitors, the rape of Provence, and the destruction of the Cathar fortress of Montségur. No wonder the Spirit departed! The attempt thereafter to restore the feminine was severely constrained, and mystics, artists, and scientists of the heretical church were forced to pursue their interests in secrecy. The disciplines of medicine, alchemy, astrology, mysticism, and psychology that had once flourished were forced underground and condemned as "occult."

But many monuments of the twelfth and thirteenth centuries still give witness to the enlightened mentality of their architects and builders. A particularly fascinating example of the "occult" geometry found in the Church of San Miniato, built in 1207 in Florence, Italy, is discussed in a recent book by Fred Gettings.[14] This church has a zodiac mosaic in the marble floor and a coded inscription that Gettings believes shows that the church was deliberately oriented toward a rare "stellium," which was the conjunction of the planets Mercury, Venus, and Saturn in the sign of Taurus that occurred at the end of May in 1207. That such accuracy of alignment was possible indicates that the secret wisdom of the ancients was available to the designer of San Miniato. Further, this alignment indicates that the practice of astrology was important in medieval Europe.

Astrology was one of the arts taught at the school at Chartres in the twelfth and thirteenth centuries. The study of astronomy enabled the learned to contemplate the laws of the heavens and the grand design of the Divine Geometer, the Creator. The casting of "foundation charts" for the cathedrals of Western Europe was an attempt to align the structures and plans for the city of God on Earth with the eternal order of the cosmos as reflected in the movements of the planets. Sacred geometry, designed to reflect the order of the heavenly bodies, is an ancient art and science that was practiced openly in temple architecture for millennia until the Inquisition forced it into occult practice.

We have discussed how the faith of the Templars, which celebrated the cosmic balance of the opposites, was built into the cathedrals. The magnificent "rose windows" of stained glass are yet another example of the resurgent feminine among the designers of the medieval churches in honor of "Notre Dame." In addition, it was the belief of medieval gypsies that the Gothic cathedrals of Our Lady in northern France were deliberately situated so as to form a mirror image of the constellation Virgo—"Our Lady"—plotted on the ground.

Although the veneration of the Bride of Jesus had been officially suppressed by the Catholic Church, shrines to the Virgin Mary continued to flourish, attracting pilgrims from all over Europe. The cult of the feminine was allowed to reach its apotheosis in the naming of Mary as the Virgin Queen of Heaven. But while the Virgin Mary adequately represents the maternal aspect of the feminine, the doctrine of her perpetual virginity implicitly denies the aspect of *wife*. Beautiful as this mother is, it is clear that someone very real and precious is missing from the Christian story. That someone is the Bride.

The Temple of the Bride

A fascinating book describing the practice of sacred geometry by the medieval Templars was published in 1991 by Henry Lincoln. In this book, *The Holy Place,* Lincoln relates that in the cradle of the heresy, the region that surrounds Rennes le Château in Provence, there are five mountains that form a perfect five-pointed star and a sixth mountain located at the precise center of the star.[15] According to Lincoln, this formation was perceived by the inhabitants of the region as a natural temple to the goddess of love. The configuration of this geographic temple prompted the landowners and nobility of the area to build their citadels and chapels according to alignments that form perfect five- and six-pointed stars on the ground. This can be seen by plotting the still-existing buildings and ruins on a map of the area, which is what Lincoln did. This book provides exciting evidence of the region's practice of sacred geometry in the cult of their Domina, the Magdalen.

When the Vatican and the French King Philip IV moved to dissolve the secret Order of the Knights of the Temple in 1307, those few who managed to escape went into hiding, some surfacing later in Scotland. Four centuries later, much of the lore of the Templars was reincarnated in the secret fraternity of the Freemasons. There is a great deal of fossil evidence that connects the modern Freemasons with the Knights of the Temple. This material is so relevant to our quest for the Lost Bride of Jesus that it deserves a closer look.

Freemasonry and the Templars

Modern Freemasonry draws heavily on the symbolism of the Temple that Solomon built on Mount Sion in the tenth century B.C. This Temple was built with the help of Hiram of Tyre, the artisan who crafted the twin pillars, the holy vessels, and the other ornamentation recorded in 1 Kings 7:13–50. Hiram was a prototype of the medieval alchemists, the "workers of metals." Whatever the connection between the Knights of the Temple, the alchemists, the craft of stonemasonry, and the later development of "speculative" Freemasonry, they share many of the same myths and secrets having to do with the restoration of equilibrium and the plan to rebuild the destroyed Temple.

The stonemasons' guild that built Chartres and other Gothic cathedrals called itself the Children of Solomon, as we have seen. Another similar epithet, "sons of the widow," figures heavily in the rituals of modern Freemasonry, providing one of the fossils that link modern Freemasons with the Grail heresy. Parsifal, the hero of the Grail poem of Wolfram von Eschenbach, is called "the son of the widow-lady." In addition to the allusion to the desolate "Widow Jerusalem" found in the Hebrew Book of Lamentations, this epithet can be seen to refer to the royal Jewish bloodline of David the King. The lineage of David is traced back to Ruth, the Moabite *widow* who accompanied her mother-in-law to Judea and later married Naomi's kinsman Boaz. King David was her great-grandson.

Curiously enough, devotees of the Mediterranean goddess Isis were also called "sons of the widow" in old references. We have already noted the artistic identification of Mary Magdalen with the goddess Isis, the "Queen of Heaven and Earth," who lamented over the mutilated corpse of Osiris and conceived his child.

The epithet "sons of the widow" seems to have been extended by those who knew of the Sangraal to include those descended from the widow of Jesus, who himself was a "shoot" or scion of David's royal line. The myth of David's preeminence and favored status continued to flourish among the families of the Templars.

Hiram of Tyre and the Twin Pillars

Hiram, the master architect of Solomon's Temple, is yet another "widow's son" (1 Kings 7:13). This biblical Hiram is prominent in the ritual of Freemasonry, and in their foundation myth and initiation rite of the third degree he is called Hiram Abiff. This Hiram of Tyre, the widow's son, cast the two brass pillars of the Temple, called Jachin ("established") on the right and Boaz ("strength") on the left (1 Kings 7:21). In Hebrew, reading from right to left, the pillars' meaning is "es-

FIGURE I. The Twin Pillars

tablished in strength." Because of the symbolism attached to them, these two pillars of Hiram become very important to our discussion of the widow of Jesus and the vine of the Davidic bloodline. They keep recurring and are found among the watermarks of the heretics, which will be discussed further in the next chapter (see figure 1).

In Masonic ritual the "foundation myth" of Hiram is a thinly disguised reference to another "master architect," who was foully murdered and his plans for the Temple lost or stolen. It is necessary to note here that the Greek New Testament actually calls Jesus not "carpenter" but *tekton* (Mark 6:3). A *tekton* was a construction engineer, someone who could design and build a house, a bridge, or a boat, as well as furniture.[16] References to the "master builder" Hiram are, by association, references to Jesus, who had the "master plan" for the City of God, which was lost after his death when his message was corrupted. Perhaps the word *tekton* was misunderstood and translated as "carpenter," then applied literally to Jesus rather than figuratively, as it was meant to have been. Perhaps it was meant to have been a symbolic reference to Jesus as the master builder and architect of the New Covenant.

The Lady Matronit

The building of cathedrals in honor of Our Lady by guilds of masons in medieval Europe can be seen as parallel to attempts by Jewish Cabalists in thirteenth-century Spain to restore the feminine counterpart of Yahweh in their own myths. Called interchangeably the

Shekinah and Matronit, she was the consort of Yahweh in the my-thologies of the Cabalists. She had been lost to Yahweh since the de-struction of their Temple in Jerusalem in A.D. 70.[17] According to this myth, the bridal chamber of their connubial union existing no longer, Yahweh must reign alone in the vault of heaven, separated from his beloved counterpart. Matronit, now homeless, wanders in exile like her people, the Jews in Diaspora. It seems that many theologians and philosophers of the Middle Ages were aware of the need to restore the neglected feminine principle to the celestial paradigm in order to restore balance to society. They applied the esoteric principle "As in Heaven, so on Earth."

The Crippled Fisher King

The medieval Jewish myth of Yahweh and Matronit echoes the theme of the Grail legends: the king is powerless and impotent with-out his consort. It is the loss of the feminine counterpart of the god that causes the wound that never heals, and the stricken wasteland reflects the woundedness of God.

In the legends, it is never stated that the lost Grail is the Bride. But the identity of the Fisher King of the Parsifal legend of Wolfram von Eschenbach is obvious: the wounded king is called Anfortas, a corruption of *in fortis*, which means "in strength." This is the Latin name for the left pillar of the Temple of Jerusalem, called Boaz in Hebrew. The name of this pillar, which is also the name of the ances-tor of King David, is a clear and obvious reference to the promises made to the Davidic bloodline, the line of the princes of Judah, that the dominion of its princes would be established forever "in strength," since Judah was the *strongest* of the twelve sons of Israel's patriarch Jacob. The name Anfortas is thus associated with the broken left pillar of the Temple of Jerusalem, which is symbolic of the broken Davidic succession.

In the story, the "Fisher King" Anfortas—that is, the Davidic "Fish-King" Jesus—can be healed only when the Grail is restored, and this will happen only when the right questions are asked. The loss of the feminine counterpart is the source of the king's wound, but the story was misunderstood by later interpreters of the legend who assumed the Grail to be an artifact, when in reality it was the lost and repudiated Bride.

CHAPTER V

RELICS OF THE HIDDEN CHURCH

The hidden Church of the Grail managed to keep alive the other version of Christianity for centuries. It was the adherents of this heresy who understood the nature of the King's woundedness and believed that only the restoration of his wife to the celestial paradigm and the story could heal the wasteland. It is perhaps time now to examine some of the places where the Grail heresy and the hidden church, eluding the long arm of the inquisitor, managed to flourish in the arts, crafts, and literature of Western Europe.

Harold Bayley's book *The Lost Language of Symbolism* was first published in 1912. It is a two-volume work that uses philology and mythology to explain symbols and emblems found in the watermarks of the early papermakers in Provence.[1] These watermarks, translucent designs pressed into sheets of paper, are found in the pages of European Bibles. Bayley's monumental work contains a wide range of comparative mythology, folklore, Scripture, and classical references. It includes more than fourteen hundred drawings of watermarks that he and his predecessor Charles-Moïse Briquet found in the pages of antique Bibles of the thirteenth to eighteenth centuries. The earliest marks date from 1282.[2]

The Albigensian heretics also manufactured these symbolic marks into the paper they used for printing the popular literature of their era. Fossils of their heresies can be found in these indelible marks. In other words, the tradesmen in paper found an ingenious way to hide their beliefs in symbols in order to protect them from the Inquisition.

Through this means, they secretly preserved emblems of their faith for centuries.

I believe that Bayley was mistaken in interpreting the heresy found in these watermarks as purely mystical. In many cases, the emblems are political as well as doctrinal, and the heresy to which many of them allude is that of the Grail.

We have already established that the southern part of France was a seedbed for the Grail heresy and for the flowering of arts and letters during the twelfth century. The watermarks from Bayley's research throw a great deal of light on the faith of the heretics, who seem to have believed that Jesus was an earthen vessel of the spirit of God and that his teachings would lead them to personal enlightenment and transformation. Many also believed that Jesus was married and that his bloodline still flowed in the veins of certain of their Provençal families. Some of the watermarks were mystical, referring to the way of personal holiness, purification, and service to others outlined in the Gospels. Yet even these were heretical teachings because they by-

FIGURE 2. The Unicorn

passed the liturgies and sacraments of the established Church of Rome. Other watermarks were heretical because they indicated a belief in a married Jesus who was the royal heir of David.

One of the most prevalent of all the emblems of the papermakers seems to have been the unicorn (see figure 2). According to Bayley, more than eleven hundred of the papermaker's marks he found depicted this mythical, one-horned beast. The intentional use of this symbol for Christ, the archetypal Bridegroom, is so important in medieval folklore that I will discuss it at length in the next chapter. For reasons of profound importance to our story, it was one of the favorite motifs in medieval Europe.

There are also numerous watermarks that depict a lion. The lion has many variations, but it was understood by the "mystics," or heretics, to be the Lion of Judah. The Lion of Judah is mentioned first in the Hebrew Bible in Genesis 49:8–10: "Judah, your brothers will praise you . . . your father's sons will bow down to you. You are a lion's cub, O Judah . . . the scepter shall not depart from Judah . . ." (*NIV*).

In 1 Chronicles 5:2, it is stated that the princes of Israel shall come from the tribe of Judah because he was the *strongest* of the twelve sons of Jacob. King David, the youngest son of Jesse, was descended from Judah through Boaz and Ruth, and Jesus was acclaimed as the "Son of

a.

b.

FIGURE 3
The Lion of Judah

David" during his triumphal entry into Jerusalem when the people shouted, "Hosanna!" and spread palm fronds before him. It is clearly stated in Revelation 5:5 that the Lamb who was slain and sits at the right hand of the everlasting God is "the lion of the tribe of Judah." It is this lion who is depicted in the watermarks of Provence: Jesus himself.

In one of the watermarks that Bayley copied, the lion has a pomegranate at the end of his tail (figure 3a); in another, his beard resembles a cluster of grapes (figure 3b). Bursting with red seeds, the pomegranate is a symbol for physical fertility in ancient religions. In the Song of Songs, the garden of the Bride and Bridegroom is described as an orchard of pomegranates. And the cluster of grapes is a clear reference to the fruit and seeds of the grape vine. This is a metaphor for the heritage of Israel in the Hebrew Scriptures: "The vineyard of the Lord is the House of Israel, and the men of Judah are his cherished plant" (Isa. 5:7).

In some cases, the fleur-de-lis is sprouting from the head of the lion. This three-pronged iris is the symbol used to identify the Merovingian King Clovis I (A.D. 466–511) and the legitimate royal bloodline of France. So a lion pictured with a fleur-de-lis sprouting from his head or forming the tuft of his tail is most likely a political reference

a.

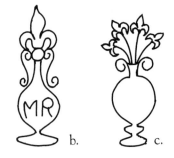
b. c.

FIGURE 4. The Grail

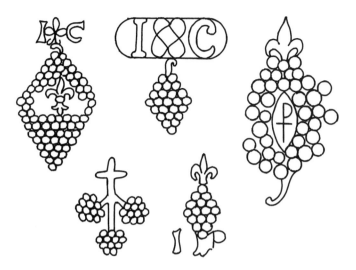

FIGURE 5. The Vine of Judah

to the royal bloodline claimed to be that of Israel and France—the line of the princes of Judah.

Other watermarks show a vessel, which Bayley calls "the Grail," often with a cluster of grapes or with several fleur-de-lis budding from it (figure 4). One of these vessels bears the initials MM for "Maria Magdalen" (figure 4a) or perhaps "Maria Maior," and another has MR for "Maria Regina" (figure 4b). Both of these epithets could just as easily apply to the Magdalen as to the virgin mother of Christ, to whom they are usually *assumed* to refer. The reference of these symbols is to the "vessel" or bearer through whom the royal line of Israel and Judah was continued. In other figures a fleur-de-lis is sprouting from a vase (figures 4b, 4c). Some emblems also show clusters of grapes that include the letters IC (for Iesu Christi in Latin) and the Merovingian fleur-de-lis (figure 5).

Another significant symbol found in the watermarks is the bear (figure 6), which was the animal connected with the Merovingians in folklore. He is the "strong one" who has been asleep for a very long time and who is expected to awaken soon—to return after his long hibernation. King Arthur's name and legend have strong associations with this Merovingian bear. In fairy tale, he appears in a story called

FIGURE 6. Merovingian Bear

FIGURE 7. Horn of the Spirit

"Snow White and Rose Red." He is under a spell cast by a wicked dwarf and must somehow break the enchantment in order to return to his true form, that of the handsome prince.

Sometimes the bear in the watermark has a "cross of light," the sign of true enlightenment, or the letters *LUX* mounted on his back (figures 6a, 6b). The six-pointed cross-of-light glyph is common to many of the watermarks. The word *LUX* was of special importance to the Albigensian heretics, whose fundamental tenet was *enlightenment*, or truth. When *lux*, the Latin word for "light," is spelled with the Greek letters ∧, ∨, and ✕, the entire word can be summed up with the single letter X, which came to designate "truth."[3] This symbol, the letter X, was held sacred because it was the mark mentioned in Latin translations of Ezekiel 9:4 with which the foreheads of the spiritually enlightened (those who mourned for Jerusalem) were to be marked. This symbol was used to mark the initiates at the Dead Sea monastery at Qumran. Later, the practice was adopted by Christians as the "sign of the cross" used in baptismal rites. I believe that this mark, the X, is an identifying Hermetic symbol of the Grail heresy and the hidden church, and that it was borrowed into the esoteric tradition in European art.

Occasionally the bear in a watermark is shown with a trumpet or horn (figures 6c through 6e). The horn is the symbol for heretical preaching (figure 7). Like the mythical horn of the French epic hero in *The Song of Roland*, its blast has the power to shatter rock. With respect to Christianity, the "rock" that heretical preaching splits is "Peter's Rock," the concretized and rigid doctrines of the institutional church. In some folklore, the horn is given the magical attribute of "making the desert bloom."[4]

In the European fairy tale of "Jack the Giant Killer," we find a golden horn that will break the enchantment and destroy the infamous ogre who holds the castle and all the people of the land in bondage. The narrative reveals that when the horn is finally blown, it will set everyone free and heal the land. One is reminded of the walls of Jericho, which purportedly fell at the trumpets' blast. In the eyes of the heretics of Provence, the Inquisition of the Roman Catholic Church was the ogre-bully. They carefully hid the tenets of their faith from its ubiquitous spies.

Another symbol found among the heretical watermarks is the Cross of Lorraine (figure 8a). It was Godfroi of Lorraine who was offered the crown of Jerusalem after the First Crusade, the knights of

Christian Europe having successfully defeated the Saracens who held the Holy City. As we discussed in the last chapter, Godfroi was alleged to be a scion of the Merovingians, whose descendants called themselves the "Vine"—the bloodline reportedly linked to Jesus. One of the objectives of the First Crusade seems to have been to install a son of that royal bloodline to the throne of Jerusalem so that the millennial promises found in Isaiah 11 could finally be fulfilled. The politics of the time seem to reflect the belief that if the royal line of David could be restored to the throne of Israel, the prophesied Millennium of the reign of God would begin.

After the defeat of the Saracens in 1099, Jerusalem was ruled for a time by the house of Lorraine. Godfroi soon sickened and died, and was succeeded by his brother Baudoin I, who accepted the title King of Jerusalem. The Holy City was later retaken by the Saracens, and subsequent Crusades attempted to reclaim it over a period of several centuries. However, the millennial hopes of the heretics did not die. Later attempts were made to put scions of the noble house of Lorraine on other thrones of Europe. The related royal family of Hapsburg-Lorraine was famous for its alliances by marriage. The Lord's word to the "shoot," or heir, of David the King is, "Not by an army, or by might, but by my spirit!" (Zech. 4:6). A wise epithet clings to the Austrian house of Hapsburg-Lorraine: "Others make war; you, happy Austria, marry!" It seems that the idea of dynastic enhancement through marriage is an old one in the case of this family that is so closely associated with the Sangraal.

The Cross of Lorraine is drawn with two crossbars instead of the

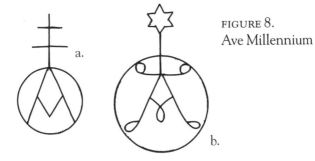

FIGURE 8.
Ave Millennium

a.

b.

usual one. The smaller bar on top represents the scroll with the inscription INRI, which stands for "Jesus of Nazareth, King of the Jews." This, the Gospels say, was posted at Pilate's command above the head of Jesus as he suffered on the cross (Mark 15:26, John 19:19), testimony to the fundamental tenet of the hidden church that Jesus was the legitimate king of David's lineage.

For centuries, the Cross of Lorraine has been used as a rallying cry for freedom in France. One of Bayley's watermarks shows an orb representing the Earth, surmounted by the double-barred cross (figure 8a). Interestingly enough, the same cross was used by the French Resistance to rally its compatriots to acts of sabotage during the Nazi occupation of France during World War II. It is also used on the membership cards of modern Freemasons, although in this case the sign is tipped on its side forming two Xs in tandem. This emblem attests to a long-standing connection between modern Freemasonry and the tenets of the Grail heresy, a connection affirmed repeatedly by the authors of *Holy Blood, Holy Grail*. The tilted emblem seems to be a coded statement: "True enlightenment *rests* with the House of Lorraine in the tenets of the Grail heresy."

The Blade and the Chalice

Bayley believes that the AVM glyph Ⱥ bears the meaning of "Ave Millennium" or "Thy Kingdom Come" (figure 8). The internal M can also be understood to stand for "Maria." The orthodox view this as a sign of "Ave Maria" and believe it to refer to the Virgin Mary, mother of Jesus. The implicit meaning of the symbol is that the millennial promises can be realized only when the Λ and the V are joined in harmony. The Λ is the archetypal masculine symbol, the "blade," and the V, its "equal opposite," is the archetype of the feminine, the "chalice." The harmony thus restored in heaven will be reflected in relationships on Earth.

At present, we have the paradigm of a perpetually bachelor son and a virgin mother as our ideal of holiness. A possible result of this combination is devaluation of the conjugal relationship of flesh-and-blood partners throughout the centuries. Yet it is the relationship of Bride and Bridegroom that is God's model for holiness, as expressed by innumerable prophets and mystics. We should note that this symbol is duplicated in the emblem of the compass and T-square of modern Freemasonry, ✕, which was once rooted in the medieval hope for the peaceful Millennium.

The letter M is prominent in many of the heretical watermarks. We have just noted the letter M formed when a V is added to the blade symbol to form the glyph for Ave Millennium, or Ave Maria. Often the letter M appears with a fleur-de-lis emerging from its center (figures 9c, 9d). Other designs that feature multiple Ms are towers and castles (figure 10). These are possible references to the Magdal, the tower or the "stronghold" of the daughter of Sion (Mic. 4:8–9). Bayley also found a number of elaborate crowns that feature the letter M (figure 11), one of them including a G for Gésu (French for "Jesus") and a horn representing the heretical preaching that shatters the "Rock" (figure 11a). This same G is prominent in the center of the compass and T-square emblem of Freemasonry, where it is now believed to refer to the word *geometry* instead of Gésu. One emblem contains the *LUX* cross and the fleur-de-lis of the royal bloodline (figure 11b) along with the initials *IC* for Iesu Christi.

Many of the watermarks have multiple Ms for Mary Magdalen and for the waves of the sea—*mare* in Latin; Miriam, the "salt sea" or "Lady of the Sea," in Hebrew.[5] The meaning of the waves is the dissolution of forms. As we know, water can come in violently destructive torrents of storm and flood, as well as in gentle streams. Even tiny ripples can cause erosion and ultimate destruction.

The heretical doctrine of Jesus' marriage, like the waves formed by the MMs (the initials of Mary Magdalen), is, I believe, understood to be linked to the sign for Aquarius. Since that sign is understood to symbolize the dissolution of forms, I suspect that the heretics hoped their doctrine of the marriage of Jesus and Mary Magdalen would erode the existing monolith of the orthodox church. It could then pave the way for an enlightened and wholesome myth in which the

FIGURE 9. The Letter M

FIGURE 10. Tower of the Flock

Earth was understood to be the partner of God, the sacred vessel that contains divinity.

This thinking makes sense even today. Restoration of the Bride, or feminine principle, in the visual paradigm of Christianity would heal the schism between spirit and matter that currently prevails, at the same time healing the wounded psyche of both male and female. The risen Jesus would no longer be separated from his Bride. The heretics seem to have believed that the restoration of the wife of Jesus would heal the wasteland and cause the desert to bloom, a motif that is reiterated in the various legends of the Grail.

The doctrines of the heretics, like those of the orthodox church, supported a myth that provided structure for their beliefs. Like the

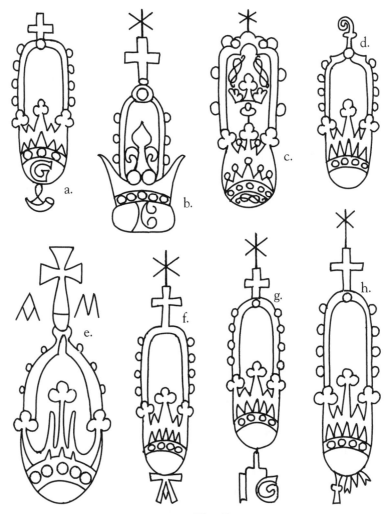

FIGURE 11. The Crown

Christian myth, the Grail heresy was securely rooted in the promises and prophecies of the Hebrew Bible. The heretics took Scripture's promises for the dynasty of David just as literally as had the Jewish people—particularly the purists and Zealots at the time of Jesus' ministry in Israel. The adherents of the Grail heresy probably believed that a ruler of the royal house of David would someday be restored to the throne of Israel and would rule the entire world with peace and justice.

In this respect, their beliefs echoed those of Judaism. The difference was that many heretics of the Middle Ages believed that the "just ruler" prophesied by Isaiah would be descended from Jesus as well as from David. He would stem from the "vine of Mary," the Merovingians. For them, the Roman Catholic Church was not the embodiment of the earthly City of God, nor was it the "New Israel," heir to the promises of the Hebrew prophets, as it claimed to be. They believed many of its doctrines to be false and adhered tenaciously to their own version of the myth of the promise. They may even have hoped that the "branch from Jesse's root" (Isa. 11:1) would eventually produce a second Messiah/King who would rule the world.

Links with Medieval Alchemy

The symbols of the medieval heretics of the Grail also seem to be linked to the tenets of alchemy found in the writings of the old spiritual masters. The alchemists' alleged search for a method of changing lead into gold through processes of chemistry and metallurgy has been widely misunderstood. Actually, the symbols for metals used in these writings were a deliberate "blind," or facade, developed to mislead the uninitiated. The system *appeared* to refer to metallurgy; thus, many aspiring scientists and gold-seekers took the words and symbols of the alchemists literally and sequestered themselves in makeshift kitchen laboratories, eventually giving birth to modern chemistry.

The actual experiments and formulas of the medieval adepts may also be linked to the staining of the magnificent colored glass that was used to create the windows of Gothic cathedrals. This art is believed to have surfaced in the eleventh century in the Middle East, just in time to be encountered there by Western Crusaders. The references of some alchemists to the colors of the heated metals (and the tinctures derived from combining and heating the metals) might very well be descriptions of the processes used in the art of glassmaking. Only the initiated could have known the formulas involved.

But the deepest and most hidden meaning of the early masters of alchemy was not chemical—it was theological, philosophical, and psychological. Their writings reveal a preoccupation with the mystical transformation of a "natural" person into a spiritually illuminated being. That natural person was called "lead," and the transformed spiritual being was called "gold." As gold is tried in fire, so the human spirit was purified in the crucible of life. The guides for the spiritual transformation were the Scriptures and certain esoteric initiations that brought enlightenment. The agent of this illumination was the Holy Spirit. This system, because it bypassed the established church and taught mystical doctrines of man's perfectibility through love and enlightenment, was deemed heretical. Consequently, the alchemists, hounded by the Inquisition, were careful to hide their faith behind the enigmatic symbols of metallurgy.

It is significant that Hiram of Tyre, the son of the widow hired to construct the Temple of Solomon in Jerusalem (1 Kings 7:13), was an artificer in metals, that is, an "alchemist." In the ancient world, knowledge of metals and their properties and alloys was a secret privilege of the royal house. It was synonymous with wealth and power. In fact, the refining of gold was the most highly valued of all state secrets. Similarly, the formulas for making stronger alloys for weapons and shinier metals for decorations that would not tarnish were carefully guarded secrets. This Hiram of Tyre, the prototypical alchemist, and Tubal Cain, "the forerunner of those who forge vessels of iron and bronze" (Gen. 5:22), are fossil links in the chain that includes the medieval alchemists, the modern Freemasons, and those remnants of the Davidic bloodline who laid claim to the epithet "sons of the widow."

The Hermetic Tradition

Another clue to this association of the medieval alchemists and modern Freemasonry can be found even in the name Hiram. Hiram has a linguistic identification with the Greek Hermes (Roman Mercury, Egyptian Thoth) who was the messenger of the gods and guardian of the crossroads, the "X." This "god of the polarities" is often pictured with winged feet and the caduceus (the emblem of the herald of the gods) and is prominent in the writings of the alchemists. Like the element mercury, or "quicksilver," he is elusive, constantly changing shape. Hermes is known as the "trickster" or "joker" because he governs the principle of synchronicity, when "meaningful coincidence" brings instant enlightenment. He seems to be a bridge that links mind and matter. This principle is understood by the alchemists to be the vehicle of transformation, and Hermes is honored as the one who brings the light.

We would need a second volume to expound on the importance of Hermes in the wisdom tradition. Hiram of Tyre, the artificer of metals and master architect of the Temple of Solomon (whose pillars, pomegranates, lily-work, nets, and vessels are described in 1 Kings), was adopted as the prototype of the enlightened alchemist, whose guide is Hermes. The foundation myth of the Rosicrucians includes the story of the "Thrice Great Hermes," Hermes Trismegistus, a legendary alchemist of Alexandria who is often pictured with triple spears representing his shafts of enlightenment. The initiates who follow his teachings are generally known as Hermeticists.

Now we will turn to other enigmatic fossils of the Grail heresy preserved in the culture of Europe. I have found that clues of the hidden heresy abound in the art and literature of Western Europe from the time of the Dark Ages and increasingly in the period following the First Crusade (A.D. 1099). Hidden references to the Grail heresy found in many formerly mysterious and misinterpreted works of art deserve careful scrutiny.

The Tarot Cards

One of the medieval artifacts that is linked by symbol to the heresy of the Lost Bride is the deck of tarot cards, the prototype for our modern decks of playing cards. The origins of the tarot are said to be obscure; speculation as to its source ranges from India to Egypt. Although tarot cards are known to have existed by the year 1392, the earliest deck still in existence is believed to have been created by a fifteenth-century painter, possibly Andrea Mantegna (1431–1506). The four suits and twenty-two "trumps" of the decks from that period definitely share symbols with the Grail heresy, and in particular the Charles VI or "Gringonneur" deck seems to have an intimate connection with the hidden tradition. Preaching against the cards in about 1450 as an invention of the devil, one Franciscan friar was particularly scathing in condemning the twenty-two trump cards, calling them "the steps on a ladder that leads to hell."[6]

When the authorities of the Catholic Church condemned the tarot cards not as immoral or decadent, but as *heretical*, they must have been fully aware of their content. I believe that the *trompes* (trumps) of the Charles VI tarot pack form a flash-card catechism for the medieval heresy of the Grail. These cards could be dated from the mid-fifteenth century, based on the costumes of the figures pictured. The stylized nimbus around the feminine figures used to portray the virtues of justice, strength, and prudence was popularized a century earlier by the Tuscan painter Giotto (1267–1337). Various dates have been suggested for the cards, but the dates are less important than the purity of the symbols on these particular cards. The artist knew exactly what he wanted to convey and consciously employed his symbols to teach the tenets of the Grail heresy. Unfortunately six of the trumps of the Charles VI deck have been lost—or more likely, expunged.

From southern France, the Grail heresy spread from court to court across Europe. I am not suggesting that the adherents of every heretical sect in Europe knew the tenets of the Grail heresy (although it is possible that many did), but in Provence, the Grail and Cathar heresies existed side by side and overlapped: many members of the aristocratic families who were linked to the Grail bloodline were also Cathars. As we have seen, the Inquisition and the Albigensian Crusade, which devastated Provence, razing castles and wiping out whole towns, were ruthless in their attempts to exterminate the heresy and the families that perpetrated it.

When Montségur, the last bastion of the Cathars, fell in 1244, the heresy went underground. Of necessity, some former heretics became outward practitioners of the faith of the establishment. It was the only survival tactic available. The heresy of the Vine, the survival of the royal bloodline of Israel, had been rooted out—or so it seemed. But in 1307, elements of the heresy were still flourishing behind the secret rites of the Knights Templar, many of whom had roots in the noble houses of Provence. When the Vatican became aware that its long-standing enemy was lurking behind the red cross of the Templars, it attempted to annihilate the entire order by decree, trying the Templars for heresy and torturing them for information about their treasure.

A century later, the tarot cards were being circulated around the courts of Europe, carried by troupes of gypsies, jokers, jugglers, and acrobats (the *jongleurs*) from town to town. Eventually they were used at playing tables in virtually every corner in Europe. The traveling entertainers had taken up where the troubadours had left off, and their symbols linger still in modern decks of cards.

The meaning of the tarot cards has been debated for centuries, with numerous revisions and interpretations ostensibly linking them to alchemy, to the secret societies of the Freemasons and Rosicrucians, and to the occult generally. The meaning of many of the cards has been declared obscure, but they retain an aura of danger. They were condemned by the church as heretical when they first made their appearance in Europe, but no one has been able to determine for sure what heresy they were hiding in their symbols. Knowledge of the Grail heresy suddenly illuminates this enigma.

A tarot deck is comprised of the Minor Arcana, consisting of four suits called swords, cups, pentacles, and scepters, and the Major Arcana (the Great Secrets) or "trumps." Our modern playing-card decks no longer have the trumps, which were the most ruthlessly condemned, although "trumping" a trick is retained in many modern card games. The only relic of the twenty-two original trumps found in our modern decks of cards is, significantly for our story, the Joker, the jester or fool reminiscent of the "clowns of God," who were credited with spreading the tenets of the Albigensian heresy. This figure is frequently found among the watermarks (figure 12). The Joker is "a fool for Christ" (1 Cor. 4:10): "We are fools for Christ . . . we hunger and thirst, we are naked and buffeted, and we have no fixed abode. We are reviled and we bless, are persecuted and we bear with it." The links with those heretics who were persecuted for the truth are clear. And even today, the Joker wins; he seems to have a hidden and irrevocable power. The Joker, by association, is also linked to Hermes/Mercury, the messenger of the gods, often called the Trickster because of his great subtlety.

Gypsies are credited with having been the source of the cards, but I believe rather that they adapted them for divination as other people adapted them for playing cards. I am convinced from the internal

FIGURE 12. The Joker

symbolism of the earliest known decks that their source was the Albigensian heresy of the Grail. It seems probable that the traveling troupes of gypsies and entertainers who accompanied the troubadours learned of the cards from the Albigensian preachers who traveled with them and taught them the tenets of the "occult" faith. To this day, it is the gypsies who throng the streets of Les Saintes-Maries-de-la-Mer in May of every year to honor Sarah the Egyptian as their dark queen.

The Trompe

The word *trompe* in Old French means "trumpet," the very same symbol of heretical preaching found among the watermarks that splits the Rock of Peter's church. It was these trumps that in the original decks illustrated the actual tenets and history of the hidden Church of the Grail. None of the authorities on the subject seems to know exactly why the trumps of the tarot deck were branded subversive, partly because the original meanings of the symbols were obscured by later copyists. Only the painters of the earliest decks knew exactly what it was they were illustrating. Later reworkings of the cards by artists who were not aware of the original meanings were often haphazard guesses or raw speculation as to the intent of the original painter of the symbols. Many of these pictures became garbled and misinterpreted along the way, just as the Grail legends took off in many directions from the basic story, until the underlying theme was all but lost in the telling.

Only the very earliest extant decks, among them the so-called Charles VI deck, retain enough of the original symbolism to identify the heresy hidden in the trumps. And so it is to this deck that we will turn in order to decipher the symbols. Let us see what the symbols found in the Charles VI trumps can tell us about the Sangraal.

The first trump card is The Simpleton, or Everyman. In Grail terminology, this is Parsifal, the uninitiated seeker. In order to be initiated into the secrets, he must ask the right questions. This path of the seeker who must ask questions is repeated in the initiation rituals of Freemasonry.

This card is followed by The Joker, which survives in modern decks. The Joker knows the secrets. He is the teacher of the Hermetic tradition. These two cards and the two following are no longer extant in the Charles VI deck, but their images can be determined by analogy with the cards of later decks.

The next card should be The Female Pope. We have already mentioned that in the heretical church, women held position and rank equal to that of men. Many were said to be descendants of Jesus; this was one of the tenets of their faith. They called themselves the Vine, referring to the royal tribe of Judah, "God's cherished plant" (Isa. 5:7). They also held sacred the line from John 14, "I am the vine, you are the branches" and from Sirach 24, "I bud forth like the vine."

According to *Holy Blood, Holy Grail*, an elite group was carefully selected and charged with passing down the secret from generation to generation. This secret cabal, called the Priory of Sion, was reputed to have been formed by Godfroi of Lorraine to protect the interests of the bloodline. Its leader, or "grand master," was elected by peers for the duration of his or her life,[7] and was always named Jean (Jeanne) after election.[8] The hidden Church of Amor was considered parallel and equal (although in opposition!) to the Church of Rome.

Four women have held the position of grand master of this Priory of Sion,[9] in effect parallel to the pope of the Roman Church. This third trump pictures The Papess, Jeanne. The church she represents is that of the Vine, the descendants of that other Mary, their royal matriarch. This other church honors the principle "seated at the left hand of God"—the feminine. It is definitely "antiestablishment." Small wonder that the card was expunged!

The next card, The Empress, is also lost; later cards show her holding a shield with a phoenix on it, but there is no way to tell if this symbol was on the Charles VI card. Clearly she was the "equal/opposite" of The Emperor (see plate 1), who appears next holding his globe and scepter, followed by the card called The Pope, seated between two cardinals in red. The pope in the Charles VI deck holds one key, reminiscent of the keys of the kingdom that the Gospel declares were given to Peter (plate 2). Presumably, the papess on the lost card held the other.

Now appears The Lovers, a card showing two cupids with ribbons forming in red the letter X across their chests (plate 3). They are aiming arrows at a procession of couples magnificently attired in the highest fashions of the day; the peers of Europe are dancing in a procession through history. This card represents the bloodline of the heresy moving in couples across the stage of Europe. The dancers are clapping and singing as they go, another subtle association with the "fruit of the vine." They are the families of the bloodline carrying the Sangraal, the Blood Royal, through the centuries. The woman in the center of the card is wearing a large and elaborate blue headdress shaped like a letter M—M for Mary? Or perhaps for Merovingian? The symbol is not accidental. The real name of this card is The Vine.

By switching the usual sequence of The Charioteer and The Hermit cards, the chronological order of the trumps is better illustrated. I suggest that the next card is the one called The Hermit, a hooded man with a long beard. The hermit shown in the Charles VI deck is Peter the Hermit (plate 4), whose zealous preaching of the First Crusade at the end of the eleventh century in Western Europe culminated in the retaking of the Holy City and its shrines. Significantly, he is holding an hourglass in the Charles VI deck, a clear reference to his theme that the time had come to liberate Jerusalem from the Saracens and to rebuild the Holy Temple. The date of the First Crusade (1098–99) was the closing hours of the first millennium after the destruction of the Temple and probably had enormous significance for the heretics, whose battle cry was, "Ave Millennium!" The large rock formation pictured on the right-hand side of The Hermit card is another confirmation of this interpretation of the card, for Peter's name, as every Christian child is taught, means "rock."

The virtues, being abstract feminine nouns, were personified by women in this tarot deck. Pictured in the next card is Strength, a woman holding a broken pillar in her arms (plate 5). This pillar is another of the keys to unlocking the meaning of the tarot cards. It represents the left pillar of the Temple of Solomon, with its "lily work" at the top. As we noted earlier, this is the pillar named Boaz (Strength) in Hebrew Scripture (1 Kings 7:21), which is associated with the Lion of the tribe of Judah and the royal Davidic succession. Boaz, the husband of the widow Ruth, was the great-grandfather of King David.

The preeminence of the descendants of Judah is described in the Hebrew Bible: "But of the race of Judah, who was the strongest among his brethren, came the princes" (1 Chron. 5:2). Boaz was of this tribe of Judah, and his direct line of descendants went through Obed, Jesse, David, and Solomon. And according to the Greek New Testament Scriptures, it culminated a thousand years later in Jesus. Boaz, the broken left pillar of the Temple, is a reference to this line of legitimate Davidic kings now broken like the pillar. The meaning here is even more graphically confirmed in the Strength card of the Mantegna tarot deck, where the woman with the broken pillar embodies two lions in her garments and a third lion stands near her: one for Judah, one for Boaz, and one for Jesus—the "thrice-strong"! Carved at the top of the pillar is a Grail design. A phrase still in current use in Masonic ritual is part of the myth of the Lost Word of the Master Builder: until the Lost Word is found in a future age, "there is strength in the Lion of Judah and he shall prevail." The Strength card represents the lineage of the Lion of Judah and the promises made to David's heirs (Ps. 89, 2 Sam. 7:16).

Now comes the card called The Charioteer in modern decks, but the man on top of the carriage in the Charles VI deck is not driving a chariot. He is a knight in armor returning victorious, holding a battle axe in his right hand and riding atop a conveyance that contains the spoils of war (plate 6). It almost looks like a hearse—or a tabernacle. His foot rests on a decoration that forms the letter I, and the next decoration, curved as it is, forms the letter C. The initials IC are the Latin initials for Iesu Christi. This trump card claims that the spoils of war brought back from Jerusalem are identified in some way with Jesus. The card portrays the return of the Templars, who are rumored to have brought back a great treasure from Palestine following the First Crusade. The Masonic ritual ceremony of the Royal Arch indicates that secret archives were dug up under the Temple of Solomon by "sojourners" in Jerusalem. Thus the famed treasure of the Temple may very well be connected to information found in the ruins of the Temple.

The tenth card, which no longer exists in the Charles VI pack but appears in other decks, is The Wheel of Fortune. I believe this refers specifically to the abrupt change in the fortunes of the Order of the Knights of the Temple. Spanning two centuries, the order amassed great wealth and political power. In the year 1307, King Philip IV of France collaborated with Pope Clement V to exterminate the Knights Templar and their order, and on Friday the thirteenth of October an edict for the arrest of the Templars was issued simultaneously in all the towns of France and throughout Europe. On that day of ill omen, the "wheel of fortune" took a radical turn against the powerful Knights Templar on whom fate had once seemed to smile so favorably.

Justice is the female virtue portrayed next (plate 7). She is holding the scales of justice and the two-edged sword. The Templars were brought to trial, accused of heresy. The Inquisition spent seven years brutally interrogating the imprisoned Templars in an attempt to discover the hiding place of their reputed treasure.

The following card, usually called The Hanged Man and said to be the most enigmatic picture in the deck, could be named The Tortured Templar (plate 8). The leg by which the Templar hangs is a metaphoric euphemism used since antiquity in literature and art in reference to the genitals. It is at the same time a subtle reference to the sacred bloodline and to the crippled Grail King Anfortas. The money bags in the hands of the hanged man represent the legendary treasure of the Temple. In spite of the unspeakable tortures of the inquisitors, the leaders of the Temple did not divulge the whereabouts of their treasure, perhaps because their real treasure was one not made of gold. Their treasure was contained in earthen vessels—the royal bloodline of Jesus the King and the other version of the Christian story, which they held in their hearts.

The trump card called Death follows (plate 9). But, strangely enough, the bodies trampled beneath the hooves of the wild ass are those of a king and the same pope and red-clad cardinals pictured on the earlier card. This is another important clue to the correct interpretation of the tarot as an Albigensian catechism: Jacques de Molay, the grand master of the Knights of the Temple, was said to have prophesied in March 1314, just before he died at the stake, that both King Philip IV of France and Pope Clement V would join him at the judgment seat of God within the year. Both died before year's end, as he had prophesied they would. This card depicts the death of the repressive establishment, the unholy alliance of the powers that collaborated to destroy the truth of the Grail and its protectors.

The next card is supposed to represent the virtue Prudence (plate 10). The female figure of the virtue sits patiently pouring water from one vessel into another. The esoteric meaning here is that the tenets that were thought to have been exterminated are carefully transferred for safety's sake into another vessel. Water is the Christian symbol for spirit and truth, the tenets of the "one true faith." They were not lost.

The Devil, which follows, is an obscene rendering of the male power principle rampant in Europe after the dissolution of the Temple and the annihilation of the Albigensians (plate 11). The figures below the hideous ogre are removing stones from his path. He is a visual representation of the "bully" of the Middle Ages, the Inquisition that was formed to root out the heresy, but which was used to quell all free thinking. The monster holds heavy chains, with which he enslaves the human race. His hideous large ears must represent the eavesdropping spies of the Inquisition who intimidated and stifled the people. It is not the heretics of the Vine who serve this evil monster; its slaves are the orthodox.

The card called The Tower pictures the destruction of a tower fortress, which is called the House of God in some later decks (plate 12).

It is a haunting reference to the Magdal-eder, the "stronghold" or "fortress" of Daughter Sion in exile. It seems to portray the destruction of the City of God that was the millennial hope and dream of the heretics. In a world that denies and represses truth, it cannot stand.

The following card is missing from the Charles VI pack, but it is called The Star in later decks. In some, a girl is pictured pouring water from two vases out onto the ground, a sign of hope for the future regeneration of the spirit and truth, which the virtue Prudence was seen pouring into a new vessel in an earlier card. The Star may also be a reference to the astrological sign of Aquarius, the water carrier, the coming age whose symbol prophesies the dissolution of the patriarchal establishment by means of the "water" of the feminine (*mare* means "the sea") and the spirit of truth. The water being poured out in this card will help the desert to bloom in the centuries to come.

In the next card, The Moon, we see the crescent moon hanging in the sky and two men at work drawing calculations on a parchment by its light (plate 18). The Moon is a prominent symbol for the occult as well as for the Goddess. These men seem to be calculating heavenly dimensions, a graphic illustration of the esoteric belief that the reality on Earth mirrors the order of the cosmos. Their measurements of the heavens will be reflected in the dimensions of the earthly Temple. The architect of the true Temple is part of the foundation myth of Freemasonry, whose rituals include Hiram Abiff and the lament "Is there no help for the widow's sons?" The motif of the building of the true Temple, in accordance with the cosmic principles of balance and equilibrium of forces, still permeates the lore of the brotherhood of Freemasons.

The men in the trump card are using the ∧ and ∨, the same shapes as the compass and T-square of later Freemasonry. Placed together these two symbols form the ideogram ⋀, the Ave Millennium found in the watermarks of the Albigensians. The exaggerated crescent moon symbolizes the occult—specifically the medieval sciences of alchemy and astrology. By many indications these sciences were linked to the building of medieval cathedrals. One could even speculate that the two men pictured in this card are establishing an astrological foundation chart for a cathedral, trying to align it with auspicious signs of the stars and the cosmos as did the builders of San Miniato. This practice was borrowed from a similar practice of Arab designers and architects during the Middle Ages.

The study of astrology seems to have been an attempt to bring the works of men into harmony with the heavenly order of the cosmos, as witnessed in the orderly progression of the planets and constellations in the sky. This was the function of the sacred geometry practiced by the wisdom schools in antiquity, and it seems to have thrived also among the architects and artists of the Middle Ages. In succeeding centuries, these arcane sciences were forced underground by the ruthless tortures of the Inquisition.

The Sun card pictures a young girl in the light of day holding a spindle (plate 14). Her hair is unbound and she is holding her thread, a symbol for continuity. She is Briar Rose, who pricked her finger on a poisoned spindle and fell asleep until a prince finally hacked his way through the briar hedge to rescue her from the evil spell. Taken with the former two cards, The Star and The Moon, we see that the water of spirit and truth poured out has become two streams that carry the tenets of the heresy. One of these, the occult sciences and secret traditions of certain societies, does so under cover of darkness (the Moon). The other stream, folktale, carries the secret in the light of day. This card alerts the seeker to look to this source for clues to the truth. The stories of the lost princess are told at every mother's knee, unchecked by the censorship of orthodoxy. The stories of women and children are not considered by the patriarchy to be important enough to be dangerous. Sometimes the safest hiding place is in the open.

Now comes Judgment Day (plate 15). Two angels are pictured blowing trumpets (again the *trompe!*), and people in the lower part of the card are rising out of their graves. The meaning here is not that of the Last Judgment conducted by the Heavenly King, part of the dogma of the Roman Church; instead, the theme is "Awake, O Sleeper!" This card pictures the day of enlightenment when all peoples will awaken to their personal responsibility and communal destiny as the one Child of God, whose name, Emmanuel, means "God is with us!" In the doctrines of the heresy, the promise is for "Reveille," not "Taps." These trumpets, like the tarot trumps themselves, are heralds of the New Day.

The final card, The World, is the fulfillment of this promise (plate 16). The righteous ruler with crown, orb, and scepter has dominion over all the Earth, enclosed in the mystic circle of perfection. The reign of God has become actual.

The Suits of the Tarot Cards

The suits of the tarot contain Grail symbolism that confirms the interpretation of the twenty-two trump cards along these lines. The suit of spades was originally a sword, the masculine "blade." Gravestones of the Knights Templar are almost invariably marked with a sword. In the original symbolism of the cards, the heart suit was a chalice. It also symbolized the Grail and the alternative church, one of whose epithets was the Church of Love. Numerous hearts appear in the Albigensian watermarks, further allying the chalice and heart motifs.

The diamond suit was originally called "pentacles," the name for a five-pointed star, which is an occult symbol for a man. According to Henry Lincoln's book *The Holy Place*, the symbol of the five-pointed star was especially significant for the alternative church and the Knights Templar. The symbol was sacred to Venus because the orbit of the planet named for the goddess of love made a perfect pentacle with relation to the sun every eight years.[10] This symbol is reflected on the ground by the five mountain peaks that form a pentagram in the heartland of the Albigensian heresy. Lincoln suggests that these were incorporated by the Knights of the Temple into a natural temple to their Lady, the Magdalen.

Perhaps most significantly of all, the club suit was in the earliest versions of the tarot a flowering rod or staff—a scepter. This symbol is the visual image of the "budding staff of Jesse's root," the messianic promise found in Isaiah 11:1 and echoed in the use of "Scepter" to refer to the Davidic Messiah in the War Scroll found among the Dead Sea Scrolls in the caves at Qumran. The trefoil club of our modern decks of cards is a clear reference to the royal lineage of Israel's kings and their divine mandate to rule. Now stylized in our modern card decks, the original emblems of the four card suits were distinct and deliberate symbols of the Grail heresy.

Throughout this discussion it is important to remember that one contribution of the Albigensians was their insistence that Scripture be translated into the vernacular. The sect was steeped in the verses of both the Hebrew and Greek Bibles. What may seem like obscure verses to us were their daily bread. This passion for direct access to the written word of God was one of their most significant gifts to Western civilization. In disseminating the Gospel, the heretics of Provence planted seeds of freedom, justice, and equality. Ultimately, these seeds became more important than the cult of the bloodline, culminating in a surge toward democracy in the eighteenth century.

Later revisions of the pictures and symbols on the tarot cards have obscured their original meanings. I have tried to reconstruct these based on the extant trumps of one of the oldest decks of cards. In light of the heresy and its connections with the Knights Templar, the symbols easily fall into a chronological sequence. By means of this "flash card" catechism, the basic tenets and history of the heresy were spread from court to court across the face of Europe. The origin and meaning of the tarot have remained a tantalizing puzzle for art historians only because they have failed to recognize its links to the Lost Bride and her intimate connection with the Albigensian heresy of the Grail.

CHAPTER VI

HERETICAL ARTISTS AND THEIR SYMBOLS

The tarot cards are only one mystery of European art that can be illuminated by the tenets of the Grail heresy. Many others exist, too numerous to mention. In this chapter I wish to comment on only a few of the painters who for centuries were believed to have been orthodox but whose paintings have symbolic content linking them irrevocably to the secret tradition, if not specifically to the heresy itself.

Two important doctrines of the alternative church were the promise of the restoration of the Davidic monarchy and the millennial promise of a world in harmony with God. The alternative church also taught enlightenment and personal transformation through the action of the Holy Spirit. The heretics did not simply believe a creed; they lived a life of personal encounter with God. Many artists and esoterics were allied with the heretics in opposition to church hegemony over European thought. And in their alliance, they were privy to the same secrets. They understood that the denial and repression of the feminine had warped and distorted their society, robbing it of ecstasy and freedom. The work of these intellectuals, most of them tied to one another in a network that transcended national boundaries, coalesced in its attempt to restore the Woman, the forgotten feminine, to consciousness.

Art scholars have recognized for centuries that the medieval masters employed symbols in their works. They have also recognized that nothing appears in their paintings that was not carefully put there to convey a meaning. The only controversy revolves around the question of what the artists really intended. Naturally, the orthodox church had its own interpretation of the symbols, but the Grail heresy and its tenets may help us understand some paintings from a different angle.

The Paintings of Botticelli

For years, art historians have sought to explain the later paintings of Sandro Filipepi. Known to the world as Botticelli, this Renaissance artist was born in 1445 and died in 1510 in Florence, the city of the de' Medici family renowned for its contributions to the rebirth of arts and letters in the fifteenth century.

The works of the young Sandro, who entered the workshop of Fra Fillipo Lippi in 1464, seem orthodox enough. However, his rendering of the Madonna and Christ Child with the two saints John, the *Bardi Madonna*, believed to have been painted about 1485, seems to be almost inexplicable, as are others from around this date and later. Some critics attribute this change to a "mystical," though undocumented, religious experience; others simply regard the late works of Botticelli as "enigmatic." Still others postulate a strong influence by the zealous monk Savonarola, who preached a wrathful judgment on Florence in a 1490 sermon.[1]

But that date is too late to explain the mystery. Beginning about the year 1483, the symbolism employed by Botticelli began to take on a character different from that of his earlier works. It has recently been suggested that Botticelli was the grand master of the secret Grail cabal called the Priory of Sion from 1483 until his death in 1510.[2] This may be key to the mystery enshrouding his later works, for the doctrines of the Grail heresy throw considerable light on enigmatic pieces believed to have been painted after that date.

We have already looked at the significance of the letter X, which conveyed to the heretics the meaning of "true enlightenment." There is evidence in other paintings that this symbol was used consciously to signal knowledge of the Hermetic or esoteric tradition. There are several incidences of a red X in the works of Botticelli, all of which, significantly I believe, were painted in or after 1483, the year when he allegedly became the grand master of the Priory of Sion.

The Madonna of the Book (plate 17) was painted in 1483. Located in almost the exact center of the picture is a red X in the bodice of the gown of the Madonna. The Christ Child is holding three small, golden spears. These may be thought to represent the nails he was to suffer on the cross, but more probably they are the esoteric symbol for the triple shafts of enlightenment, a popular motif of medieval alchemists and Rosicrucians. In another work, The Madonna of the Pomegranate (plate 18), the version Botticelli painted after 1483 shows the angel on the far left wearing red ribbons across its breast. In an earlier treatment of this same theme, Madonna with Eight Angels, believed to have been painted in 1477, all the angels have their backs turned and no crossed red ribbons are shown. It seems that in the later version, Botticelli deliberately turned the angel on the far left (the feminine side!) toward the viewer and painted the red X across its chest in full consciousness of its esoteric meaning.

Another strange item found in works attributed to Botticelli after the year 1483 is the pomegranate. In several works, Madonna of the Magnificat (plate 19), Madonna of the Pomegranate (or Madonna with Six Angels), and their variants, the baby Jesus is holding a partially opened pomegranate, an ancient symbol for physical, sexual fertility because of its profusion of red seeds. These are clearly visible in these paintings. (The pomegranate also has erotic connotations in the scriptural Song of Songs, where the lovers tryst in the orchard of pomegranates.) Later interpreters, believing Botticelli to have been a pious and ardent Roman Catholic, insist that the pomegranate is a symbol for everlasting life. Yet pictures speak louder than words. From the position of the pomegranate in the lap of the baby Jesus in several of these paintings, it appears more likely that Botticelli believed in the physical fertility of Jesus.

The Bardi Madonna, believed to have been painted in 1485, depicts a Madonna and child with Saint John the Baptist on the left and

Saint John the Evangelist on the right. In the background are bowers of cypress, olive, and palm branches. Bowls of red and white roses and vases of fruiting olive branches stand on pedestals. Intertwined among the branches are ribbons with written references to Sirach 24:14–17: "I am exalted like the cedar in Lebanon, like the cypress on Mt. Harmon, like a palm tree in Engeddi, like a rosebush in Jericho, like a fair olive tree in the field . . . I spread out my branches like a terebinth . . . *I bud forth like the vine*" (emphasis added). Knowing that the descendants of Jesus called themselves the Vine helps to interpret this painting in a new light. Here, the baby looks as if he is about to fall off the his mother's lap. All the figures seem distorted, especially John the Baptist, who looks as if he is in anguish as he points toward the baby Jesus. The ribbon he holds says Ecce Agnus Dei: "Behold the Lamb of God." To the heretics, Jesus was the Lamb of God, who was brutally butchered by the Romans, led to the slaughter as prophesied in Isaiah. In Revelation 5, the Lamb is worthy of praise and honor, glory and riches, and sits at the right hand of God. But according to the heretics, the Lamb is not the same as the unseen God who sits upon the throne of heaven. Worship God alone!

The importance of John the Baptist to the heretics is easy to understand. First of all, he is their cousin. His relationship to Jesus is one of flesh and blood, since Scripture says that his mother, Elizabeth, was cousin to Mary the mother of Jesus. John the Evangelist is equally honored by the hidden church. The Cathari wore a copy of his Gospel concealed under their garments on a cord tied around their waists as they journeyed to their secret meeting places. In this favorite Gospel, John the Baptist greets Jesus as "Lamb of God" and baptizes him in the River Jordan. There occurs a passage in John's Gospel (3:29) that quotes John the Baptist explaining his relationship with Jesus: "He who hath the bride is the bridegroom; but the friend of the bridegroom who stands and hears him, rejoices exceedingly at the voice of the bridegroom. This my joy therefore is made full." This passage is not merely an analogy. In this text, John the Baptist names his cousin Jesus the surrogate Bridegroom of Israel.

PLATE 1. The Emperor

PLATE 2. The Pope

PLATE 3. The Lovers

PLATE 4. "Peter the Hermit"

PLATE 5. Strength

PLATE 6. The Charioteer

PLATE 7. Justice

PLATE 8. The Hanged Man

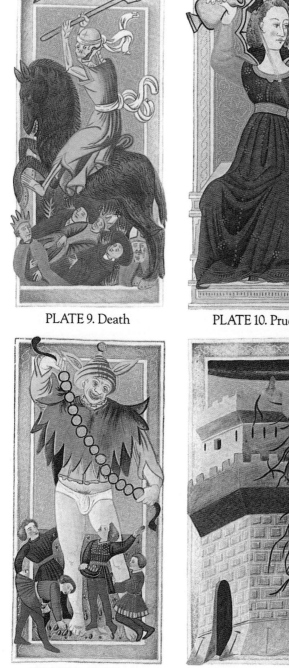

PLATE 9. Death

PLATE 10. Prudence

PLATE 11. The Devil

PLATE 12. The Tower

PLATE 13. The Moon

PLATE 14. The Sun

PLATE 15. Judgment

PLATE 16. The World

PLATE 17. Madonna of the Book by Botticelli, Museo Poldi Pezzoli, Milan

PLATE 18. Madonna of the Pomegranate *by Botticelli, Uffizi, Florence*

PLATE 19. Madonna of the Magnificat *by Botticelli, Uffizi, Florence*

PLATE 20. Saint Mary Magdalene at the Foot of the Cross *by Botticelli, The Fogg Art Museum, Cambridge*

PLATE 21. Derelicta *by Botticelli, Pallavicini Rospigliosi, Rome*

PLATE 22. Saint Mary Magdalen *by della Francesca, Arezzo Cathedral,*
Fresco

PLATE 23. Noli Me Tangere *by Fra Angelico, Museo de S. Marco, Florence*

PLATE 24. The Penitent Magdalen by *Georges de la Tour*, The Metropolitan *Museum of Art, New York*

PLATE 25. The Hunt of the Unicorn, Panel VII, "The Unicorn in Captivity," *The Metropolitan Museum of Art, New York*

PLATE 26. La Dame à la Licorne, "Sight," *Musée de Cluny, Paris*

PLATE 27. La Dame à la Licorne, "Touch," *Musée de Cluny, Paris*

PLATE 28. Road to Calvary *by Simone Martini, Louvre, Paris*

Modern Freemasons, whose secret brotherhood traces many elements back to the Knights Templar and whose rituals and symbols reflect elements of the heresy, chose these same two saints as their patrons.[3] As mentioned, each grand master of the Priory of Sion takes the name Jean (John) upon election to that office.[4] These two saints, John the Baptist and John the Evangelist, clearly have special significance for the followers of the esoteric tradition and the alternative church.

Let us look now at a painting entitled *Saint Mary Magdalene at the Foot of the Cross* (plate 20), painted by Botticelli in about 1500. Here the desolate figure of Mary Magdalen clings to the foot of the cross on which Jesus hangs. On the right is a figure of an angel gripping a fox, which he holds upside down by the tail. Dark storm clouds in the painting are being driven away, and from the nimbus in the upper left corner, where God the Father is pictured blessing the scene, angels are descending from the sky, each bearing a shield of white with a tilted red X emblazoned on it. It almost seems as if Botticelli delighted in finding new ways of including the red X in his paintings!

In this painting, it appears as though the angels with the red crosses are dispelling the darkness that enshrouds the relationship between Jesus and Mary Magdalen. The fox is a Gnostic symbol for pious fraud. Popular stories and pictures from the Middle Ages often depict a fox dressed in a monk's robe, going slyly about his business of deceiving and exploiting the people. For them, the clergymen of the Roman Church were "foxes." Reference to foxes is found in the favorite scripture of the heretics, the Song of Songs, in which the "little foxes" spoil the vines in the vineyard of the Bride (Cant. 2:15). The fox in the painting represents the fraud perpetuated by the orthodox church, which insisted that Jesus had been celibate. This belief was, in effect, "spoiling the vine" by denying the legitimacy of the bloodline. The tilted red crosses on the shields of the angels, echoing the emblem of the Knights Templar, denote the protection of the true "vine" by the Priory of Sion and its militant arm, the Knights of the Temple. Interpreted along these lines, this painting becomes a reflection of the tenets of the Grail heresy, of which Botticelli is claimed to have been chief custodian at the time this masterpiece was painted.

One of the most eloquent of all Botticelli's paintings is the *Derelicta* (plate 21), painted about 1495. Numerous critics have tried to guess the identity of the desolate woman huddled on the steps before the closed door, shreds of her rose-colored cloak scattered around her. No one seems to have recognized the "Derelicta" as the bride from the Song of Songs, beaten by the guardians of the walls who took her mantle. She is the scorned and wounded feminine, barred from full participation in the community. Her name in Latin means "abandoned."

In addition to Botticelli, there are numerous other painters of the Middle Ages whose works indicate a knowledge of the Grail heresy. When examining the religious paintings of these artists, it is important to distinguish carefully between those who used the secret symbols in a conscious attempt to promote the heresy and those who merely copied symbols whose significance they did not fully understand.

Paintings of the Madonna and Child were numerous in Europe during the late Middle Ages, and they provide fertile ground for our investigation. Clearly, the feminine was a favorite subject for artists, both orthodox and heretical. And many of the paintings illustrate an esoteric or heretical understanding of Christ through use of Hermetic symbols. Some artists who were believed to be orthodox left symbols in their paintings that belie their supposed affiliations. Again, a knowledge of the meanings of colors and symbols is the key.

The Paintings of Fra Angelico

The paintings of Fra Angelico have always seemed to be entirely orthodox. But on close examination, many can be shown to contain the conscious use of esoteric symbols. This should not surprise us when we remember that this monk was a citizen of Florence in the mid-fifteenth century at precisely the time when heresy was most rampant in that city.

In one of his paintings of the Madonna and Child, Mary is holding two roses, one red and one white. The red and white are the colors of the Sister-Bride, red representing passion and white representing purity. For alchemists, red and white symbolized the "union of the opposites." To the orthodox believers, purity and passion were mutually exclusive and antithetical, but among the heretics of the hidden church, they were united in the Sister-Bride. Accordingly, bowls, baskets, garlands, and wreaths of alternating red and white roses occur often in the paintings of Fra Angelico, Botticelli, and other Hermeticists.

To expand a little on this color symbolism, a work painted by Piero della Francesca in about 1466 presents a massive figure of the Magdalen in a gown of green, the color of fertility (plate 22). Over the gown she wears a red cloak that is folded back to display an accentuated white lining. This white lining emphasizes her purity, in contrast to the tradition that names her prostitute. We cannot avoid focusing on the white lining of the scarlet cape. The color red or rose is most often associated with Mary Magdalen in medieval paintings (only occasionally is she dressed in green). The Inquisition became so upset with pictures of the Madonna dressed in red that its art censor finally decreed in 1649 that all paintings of the Virgin Mary would be rendered in blue and white, acknowledging the sister and mother aspects of the eternal feminine, but denying the bridal or flesh-and-blood sexual aspect. Paintings of Madonnas wearing red were strictly forbidden, and the "woman in red" became synonymous with a woman of the street.

The "tri-color"—red, white, and blue—has a familiar sound, and its origins are older than recorded history. The Triple Goddess common to ancient religions of Europe, Africa, and the Near East before the Indo-Aryan invasions had three aspects: maiden (sister), bride (spouse, childbearer) and old woman (crone or hag). Her colors corresponding to these aspects were white, red, and dark blue or black.[5] Thus the Triple Goddess combines all three aspects in her worldwide cult of the feminine. However, in the Christian myth articulated by the orthodox church, her bridal "flesh-and-blood" aspect is traditionally denied.

Perhaps the most significant painting of Fra Angelico that seems to contain a hidden reference to the Grail heresy is a painting on the wall of the first cell in the San Marco Convent in Florence (plate 23). The famous mural is called *Noli Me Tangere* ("Do not Touch Me"). The title is taken from the Gospel of John 20:17. Jesus is standing in the enclosed garden with a hoe over his shoulder, a symbol emphasizing his role as husbandman, the "gardener" of the Fourth Gospel. Kneeling at his feet and reaching out toward him is Mary Magdalen, dressed in a rose-colored gown. Under her left hand, painted unobtrusively among the flowers in the grass, are three tiny red Xs in a row.

The red X, the secret esoteric symbol of the heretical church, was the antiestablishment symbol for truth. It signaled the fundamental flaw in orthodox Christian doctrine: the denial of the wife of Jesus. The triple Xs under the left hand of the Magdalen refer to the secret doctrines. In the picture, her right hand is pointing directly toward these Xs. Yet they could be claimed to be accidental. Several other works by Fra Angelico have red and white flowers sprinkled in the grass, but none I have seen other than the *Noli Me Tangere* have three Xs painted side by side.

If these three tiny Xs occurred anywhere else in the picture they might be accidental, but because they occur under the left hand of Mary Magdalen, a clear association with the maternal, or "bar sinister," side of the royal bloodline, I believe they are a clear case of conscious symbolism. Today *bar sinister* has taken on the pejorative meaning of an illegitimate bloodline. But its original meaning in the heraldry of the Middle Ages was the lineage of the mother of the shield bearer. Her coat of arms was emblazoned on the left-hand side of the shield with the father's family symbols painted on the right.

The military significance of using painted shields to identify battlefield commanders was apparent to Crusaders, who encountered the practice among the Saracens and adopted it for their own shields beginning in the twelfth century. The feminine was identified with the left hand, the masculine with the right. This terminology has been carried into the field of modern psychology, where the left-brained, right-handed orientation is considered "masculine" and "rational" and the right-brained, left-handed orientation is labeled "feminine" or "artistic/intuitive." One is *dexter*, the other *sinister*. The same dualistic "head" and "heart" associations are carried into the political arena, where the "right" is conservative and the "left" is liberal.

It should not surprise us that the painters and scholars of Florence were steeped in the esoteric traditions of the secret cult and its heresy. Cosimo de' Medici established his extensive library of classical Greek, Latin, and Arabic writings there during the mid-fifteenth century, in spite of the repressive influence of the Inquisition. The city was a fertile field for sophisticated artists and poets, and they flocked to it as an enlightened center. The study of classical literature, alchemy, and esoterica flourished in these circles and spread to intellectuals in all corners of Europe.

Other Suspicious Symbols in Art

One painting of the Disposition painted by an unknown medieval artist and now displayed in the Louvre shows Mary Magdalen in what is known as the "Astarte" pose: she is holding her breasts cupped with her hands. This pose is most commonly found in statues of the Middle Eastern fertility goddess, who is the consort of the sacrificed sun god. Surely this painting is at least slightly surprising!

In another supposedly orthodox sixteenth-century painting by an anonymous German master, Mary Magdalen is depicted with a black glove on her left hand. This is a clear reference to the maternal bloodline and to the Widow Sion, whose sons are black and "not recognized in the streets" (Lam. 4:8). In this painting, the palm of Mary's hand is prominent. The watermarks of Provence make frequent use of the palm of the hand as an important symbol (figure 13). Its meaning is, "maintain the faith, the promise of the Davidic Messiah!"

The "palm" tree is also a significant symbol of Israel and the house of King David. It refers to the Gospel passages in which the people

FIGURE 13. The Palm

spread palms before Jesus, welcoming him as the son of David when he rode the donkey into Jerusalem. In Greek, the word for palm tree is *phoenix*. Even this pun has medieval associations with Jesus. The mythical "palm" bird is said to have risen from its own ashes and was a symbol of resurrection. Bayley's watermarks are taken from Bibles found in other European languages as well as French, so these word plays should all be taken into account when interpreting them.

The works of the Italian painter Carlo Crivelli (1430–1493) also seem to contain conscious use of esoteric symbolism. Several portrayals of the Madonna and Child depict a cracked wall with a fly on it. The crack in the wall represents, I believe, the flawed edifice of orthodox doctrine, while the fly suggests corruption. Above the Madonna's head is a cluster of fruit that includes one prominent green cucumber. The reference here may be to the lament of the Hebrew prophet Isaiah that the daughter of Sion is left as a "shelter in a vineyard, a hut in a garden of cucumbers, a city besieged" (Isa. 1:8). Bayley's watermarks include gourds and cucumbers that illustrated this lament. This symbolism refers not to the *orthodox* church but to the exiled daughter of Sion, the alternative hidden Church of the Grail, the "city under siege." This painting should have made the inquisitors shudder.

Another Crivelli rendering of the Madonna and Child, painted about 1473, shows the pair enthroned with carved fish on either side of the throne, a reference to the astrological Age of Pisces, the Age of the Fishes. Jesus was understood by medieval Hermeticists and alchemists to be Lord of the Piscean Age of the astrological zodiac, the bearer of the sign of the fish.[6] (See figure 14.)

Many medieval and Renaissance paintings of the Nativity of Jesus show a grotto, a poor shelter or cave in a hillside, surrounded by crumbling pillars of buildings and temples of the classical age. These paintings illustrate the understanding that the birth of Jesus coincided with the dissolution of the former age and the birth of the new. In Matthew 2:2, the Magi report having seen the star of the Babe when it rose in the east. The word magi means "wise men, priests, or astrologers," and the new constellation rising at the time of Jesus was Pisces. A prime example of the theme of the dying age being superseded by the new is found in Botticelli's *Adoration of the Magi*, where the makeshift shelter over the nativity scene is surrounded by the crumbling pillars of the Hellenistic empire.

Saint Mary Magdalen, a painting completed in 1528 by the Dutch master Jan van Scorel, depicts Mary Magdalen with a large urn or vase, similar to those portraying the Grail in the watermarks. She is sitting near the old broken stump of a gigantic tree, and its one live branch is bearing leaves above her head. The left sleeve of her gown is decorated with rows of pearls forming Xs. Bordering the neck of the gown are embroidered Hebrew letters, indicating her national origins. The pearl is often associated with Mary Magdalen, I believe, be-

FIGURE 14. Merovingian Fish

cause the "pearl of great price," like the Grail itself, is something of utmost value that needs to be sought.

Another painter who associates the pearl with Mary Magdalen is Georges de la Tour (1593–1652). This artist was a native of Lunéville in Lorraine. He painted six different versions of *The Penitent Magdalen* (plate 24). In each version, the woman is wearing a white blouse and a red skirt, the red and white of the Sister-Bride, symbolic of passion and purity combined. She is seated in a chair gazing at various items—a skull, a candle, a mirror, or a large pearl. The woman is invariably pregnant.

I find it amusing that the term *sub rosa* implies something done in secret. The idiom "under the sign of the rose" actually meant something specific for the initiated. For them, as we have seen, the secret *is* the rose—the red rose of the other Mary, the Mary who represents Eros, the passionate *bridal* aspect of the feminine, which was denied by the established church. Eros is an anagram for rose, and the rose has been sacred to the love goddesses since antiquity.

The Rosicrucians, whose secret societies proliferated during the seventeenth century but probably originated much earlier, used the symbol of a rose-colored cross. The full meaning of this cross was probably known only to a small number of initiates. This was not the orthodox cross of Peter and Jesus, the † that was repudiated by the heretics as a despicable instrument of torture. Their cross was the red X of true enlightenment, symbol of *lux* or "light." Yet because their version of the life and nature of Jesus was at odds with that of the orthodox church, it was "rated X," condemned, and repudiated.

The pejorative meaning of the letter X in modern usage—that is, "X-rated movies" or answers marked wrong on a test—is evidence of the power of the victor to demolish the vanquished and rewrite the record. The establishment discredited the X and made it anathema to the community. But an even earlier use of the letter X was on documents in lieu of signatures. We can almost picture a tortured heretic being forced to sign his confession and instead choosing to mark it with an X. This is exactly the sort of wily "disinformation" that prisoners of the faith would have found gloriously ironic.

Saint Andrew's Cross

The prevalence of the X symbol in the Middle Ages and the meanings it conveyed should not be passed over lightly. At some point, the letter X became associated with the term "antiestablishment." In the fourteenth century, a legend concerning this cross was circulating in Europe, perhaps due to the story in Jacobus de Voragine's thirteenth-century *Golden Legend*, which was then popular. It was said that Saint Andrew had been martyred on an equilateral cross tilted sideways. This legend seems to have been an attempt to legitimize the esoteric X that was being used in paintings—the X that bore the meaning of *lux*. The saint chosen for the honor of being associated with the X was the Apostle Andrew, who met Jesus first and then ran to find his brother Peter. The legend seems to be an attempt to give the X associated with Saint Andrew precedence over the † venerated in Peter's church.

Saint Andrew, because he knew Jesus first, would have had a certain priority over Peter. Peter's name means "Rock"; Andrew's comes from *andro*, meaning "man," a contrast that cannot have been overlooked by the heretics. Saint Andrew became the patron saint of Scotland, reputed to have been the haven of the Templars following the purge of their order in 1307.[7] His cross is still found in the flag of Great Britain superimposed on the cross of the orthodox church.

Another favorite saint often associated with the X was Saint George, called the "Red Cross Knight." Saint George is invariably depicted holding a white shield bearing a red cross. He is credited with having slain the dragon and rescued the damsel in distress. The "beast" is always a threat to the "woman" (Rev. 12:6), and the red cross is associated with her rescue (as it is today a symbol for emergency aid; our symbols run deep in our consciousness and keep re-emerging). European Crusaders first encountered the fertility cult of Saint George in

the eleventh century during their sojourn in the eastern cities of Byzantium. In the folk tradition of the Red Cross Knight, Saint George
is called the "ever-green one," and he is the patron of barren women.
The healing of the barren land and the "scorched earth" is invariably
associated with the red X!

The two saints of the X were universally popular in Europe. A
third saint who often bears a shield with a red cross is Saint Michael
the archangel, another champion of the "woman" (Rev. 12:7), who finally defeats the "beast." Michael, "the living image of God," is often
identified with the god Hermes in Christian iconography. Many medieval painters seem to have deliberately included Michael, Andrew,
or George in their paintings, perhaps so that they would have a good
excuse to include the red code letter X, the "rosy cross," in their works.

Of course, not every artist used the symbol consciously, but many
seem to have included it as a way of flaunting their true allegiance under the very nose of the Inquisition. In a way, it was like prisoners of
war tapping the opening line of the Twenty-third Psalm or the national anthem in Morse code to communicate hope to one another
while in captivity. Or like the opening words of Pope John Paul II in
his inaugural address in October 1978: "When the moon shines over
Czestochowa"—the first line of an intensely patriotic Polish poem
that secretly carried to Polish freedom fighters a thrilling message of
hope. Similarly, the red X in medieval art proclaimed unwavering solidarity with the heretical secret tradition. It seems almost unneces-
sary to point out that both the heretics of the Grail and the activists
of the anti-communist Solidarity movement during the 1980s in Poland held sacred the image of the Black Madonna. She has been the
beloved patroness of freedom fighters for two millennia!

Certainly many designers of watermarks in Europe were strictly
orthodox, just as many of the religious painters were. And many troubadours merely copied the motifs and phrases of the earlier singers.
One has to go back to the early examples and examine them carefully,
as we did the Tarot cards, to determine which artists were consciously

promulgating the doctrines of the heresy. But the evidence suggests that many prominent artists and poets deliberately flagged their work with signs of their Lady, the Magdalen. And the Inquisition, not knowing what to look for, overlooked the Xs and rationalized many other symbols to fit their doctrines as best they could. But everyone with eyes to see must realize that a pomegranate bursting with bright red seeds is not a spiritual symbol, especially when it is resting in someone's lap!

The origin of the red X as a pejorative symbol for sexually explicit material stems, it seems, from the hidden Church of the Grail and its adherents. It is as if the orthodox church associated the letter X with the temptations and sins of "the world, the flesh, and the devil"— summed up as always in the feminine, the occult, and the "sinister." But the archaic meaning of the X, the union of the male and female in holy and equal partnership, is inherent in its very structure: a combining (or "nuptials") of the ancient and archetypal V, the feminine chalice, and ∧, the masculine blade.

THE UNICORN AND THE LADY

Our themes of the Sacred Marriage and the Lost Bride in Western culture have led us to explore enigmas in medieval art that might be illuminated by the tenets of the Grail heresy. Among these artworks must be included the fabulous unicorn tapestries that are relics of the late Middle Ages. It has been suggested that the tapestry series called *La Dame à la Licorne* in particular illustrates an unspecified doctrine of the Cathars.[1] I am convinced that it was the Albigensian Grail heresy that inspired the artist to design this subtle masterpiece—in honor of the Bride.

Scholars of the subject agree that the unicorn was a mythical animal mentioned in classical times by the Greeks Ctesias of Cnidos and Aristotle and by the Roman historian Pliny, among others. No one seems quite sure of the source of the myth, but Bronze Age mural paintings (2000–1500 B.C.) of antelope in profile look very much like the mythical unicorn, because the second horn is not visible behind the first. This is one possible source of the legendary horselike creature with one horn protruding from his forehead. The *Physiologus*, a bestiary written in the third century A.D. in Alexandria, compiled myths of various species. It included the ferocious unicorn, which could not be captured by hunters but which could be lured to the side of a virgin and captured as it slept with its head in her lap. The *Physiologus* was widely translated for more than one thousand years and its legends circulated throughout Christendom.

The early church patriarchs recognized the unicorn as a figure of Christ, a tradition that carried into medieval times, when the unicorn was believed to have special powers of healing. Powders ground from the animal's mythical horn were part of every pharmaceutical store. The story was often repeated that the unicorn could purify poisonous waters by dipping his magical horn into them. Some renderings of the unicorn in medieval art show the unicorn dipping his horn into a stream or fountain, while others portray him with his head in the lap of a maiden, who is usually shown against a flowery background or seated in an enclosed garden. The unicorn is one of the most frequent of all the recurring symbols among the Albigensian watermarks. For this reason, if for no other, we should examine examples of this motif in art and legend.

While medieval apologists for orthodoxy strove to give the unicorn legend mystical meaning, the connotations of the garden and the imagery of the beast with the horn in the maiden's lap are indisputably linked to the Song of Songs. Orthodox interpreters tried to equate the enclosed garden with the virginity of Mary, the mother of Jesus, but that is clearly not what was meant in the biblical reference to the "garden enclosed" found in the song: "You are a garden enclosed, my sister, my bride" (Cant. 4:12), and "I have come into my garden, my sister, my bride" (Cant. 5:1). The entire song extols the delights of the senses—the fragrances, tastes, sights, and sounds of the "garden" where the lovers are united. Their couch is the grass: "Our bed is verdant" (Cant. 1:15).

The church, in the Judaic tradition, has insisted for centuries that this canticle of the archetypal lovers is a mystical allegory, but we have already noted that its erotic imagery is similar to that of the ritual poetry of the Sacred Marriage in the Near East. I am convinced that the lady in the garden of the unicorn tapestries is the Sister-Bride of the Song of Songs. This does not preclude a mystical interpretation of the tapestry or of the song; it only precedes and enhances it.

La Dame à la Licorne

The tapestry *The Lady and the Unicorn* displayed in the Cluny Museum in Paris extols the feminine and the delights of the senses. The lady in the six panels of the tapestry is shown against a red background covered with tiny flora and fauna of every description, including numerous bunnies, which, because of their reputation for fertility, were sacred to the goddess of love. The lady is dressed in floral brocades with ornate jewels and hair styles of the late fifteenth century. She is holding a mirror, a symbol most frequently associated with Venus/Aphrodite, in which the unicorn is reflected. Flanking her in each panel of the tapestry are the lion (of Judah) and the unicorn, both medieval symbols for Christ.

In the first panel of the tapestry (plate 26), the unicorn has raised the lady's skirt and has his hooves resting comfortably in her lap! The lion and the unicorn are each holding a banner of red, white, and dark blue, the colors of the Triple Goddess. These banners are red, with three white crescents on a dark blue band. Since the waxing crescent moon is a symbol for the "maiden," these banners proclaim that the lady is the Sister-Bride awaiting her Bridegroom in the garden.

Even the banners in the tapestry have a haunting association with the Song of Songs: "His banner over me is love" (Cant. 2:4, *NIV*). In the song, the Bride is invited to a banquet of the senses, and the one who holds the banner of love is her Bridegroom. Some scholars have suggested that this tapestry may have been designed as a wedding gift for a particular bride, possibly a daughter of the La Vista family from the Lyons area of Southern France, whose heraldic device was three crescent moons similar to those on the banners.[2] I am inclined to think that the La Vista family became associated with this crest because they already owned the marvelous tapestry with its distinctive banners. The same band with three crescents appears in the coat of arms of Lunéville, a city in Lorraine.

The symbolism of the tapestry provides a delightful bouquet for the five senses, extolling each in turn.[3] The first panel, in which the lady holds the mirror, illustrates "Sight." In the second, labeled "Sound," she is playing an organ. In the third, called "Taste," she is taking a sweet-meat from a dish. In "Smell," the fourth panel of the series, the lady is fashioning a wreath of carnations while her handmaiden holds a container of periwinkle blossoms. Medievalist and horticulturist John Williamson did a detailed study of the flora symbolism of the unicorn tapestries displayed at the Cloisters of the Metropolitan Museum of Art in New York. According to his research, the carnation was a medieval symbol for betrothal and the periwinkle a symbol for marriage.[4] The individual plants and flowers of the unicorn tapestries were woven with such extreme deliberation that each one can be recognized.

In his book *The Oak King, the Holly King and the Unicorn*, Williamson notes that many of the trees and plants of the unicorn tapestries are used to aid fertility (wallflower, stock gillyflower, daisy, violet) or are aphrodisiacs (cuckoopint, periwinkle, and male orchid). His fascinating study is based on the herbals and natural histories of the Middle Ages, their legends and lore. While Williamson's book deals explicitly with the seven panels of the unicorn tapestries exhibited at the Cloisters, similar flora and fauna are found in the tapestries of the Cluny Museum, and the tapestries of both series are presumed to have been woven at approximately the same date near the end of the fifteenth century, most likely in the Flemish city of Brussels. It is believed that the cartoons were designed by a French artist, but his/her name is unknown. Appearing in several panels of these tapestries are the carnation (betrothal), the violet (lust), the rose (love), and the periwinkle (marriage) along with the trees of oak (solar principle), holly (lunar principle), orange (conjugal union of the sexes), pomegranate (female fecundity), and pine (male fertility).[5]

Some interpreters see these panels as portraying a medieval courtship or perhaps the cult of courtly love. It is clear that the progression of these panels becomes more intimate. In the fifth panel, "Touch," the Lady is caressing the horn of the unicorn (plate 27). She is now holding the banner herself, and the rabbit at her feet is playing with a tiny red flower shaped like an X. This could be accidental on the part of the artist, but I very much doubt that it is. The lady in these panels is the Dompna of the troubadours, the Beloved. She is also, of course, the prototype of the soul of which Christ is the mystical Bridegroom. The ecstasy of mystical marriage is foreshadowed in the physical world. Thus, the tapestries may be intended to mirror both transcendent and earthly reality.

The sixth panel shows a dark blue tent, held open by the lion and the unicorn, still bearing the banners of the Sister-Bride. The lady has taken off her necklace and is handing it to her waiting-woman. The necklace is also mentioned in the Canticles: "You have ravished my heart with one glance from your eyes, with one jewel of your necklace" (Cant. 4:9). Above the tent, which represents the sanctuary, appear the words A mon seul desir. The tent is the bridal chamber of the Sacred Marriage, where the Bride awaits her Bridegroom: "Let my lover come into his garden and taste its choice fruits" (Cant. 4:16).

The Bridegroom of Israel

The unicorn is mentioned in the Ninety-second Psalm in the Greek version of the Bible, the Septuagint: "My horn shalt thou exalt like the horn of the unicorn; I shall be anointed with fresh oil." This text associates the unicorn with the anointing of the king and is an echo of the line from the Twenty-third Psalm, where the king addresses the feminine deity: "You anoint my head with oil, my cup overflows." Perhaps on the basis of this association of the horn of the unicorn with the anointing of the king, the unicorn was an ancient emblem of the kings of Israel.

The line may also be the source of the widespread association of the mythical beast with Jesus Christ, the anointed Messiah of Israel. All the prophecies and psalms of the Davidic Messiah in the Hebrew Bible were understood by the exegetes of early Christianity to refer to Jesus as well. The anointing of the "horn" or "head" of the Bridegroom/King was a part of the ancient ritual of the hieros gamos. Of course, the medieval church would have ignored the sexual connotations of the single raised horn and stressed the symbolism of strength and purity instead. But it does seem strange that the unicorn of the legend is lured to place his head in the lap of a virgin.

Poetry for the ritual of the *hieros gamos*, written in ancient Sumer to the love goddess Inanna, includes these lines:

> The king goes with lifted head to the holy lap,
> He goes with lifted head to the holy lap of Inanna,
> The king coming with lifted head
> Coming to my queen with lifted head . . .[6]

The Bridegroom/King with "lifted head" or "horn" inevitably seeks the lap of the Bride for the consummation of the Sacred Marriage. So does the mythical unicorn. The erotic meaning of the imagery should not be ignored. Although the tapestries were woven at the dawn of the Renaissance period (A.D. 1500), the story of the unicorn with his head in the lap of the maiden originated in the classical world, where the imagery of the sacred king and his marriage to the love goddess was familiar.

The most important attribute of the sacred king was virility, and his most important function was to protect his realm. Later this translated into the ability to beget sons. Without heirs, a king was considered weak, and the future of his kingdom was insecure. This physical reality applied to the kings of Europe just as intensely as it did to kings in earlier times. Undoubtedly the medieval world understood the erotic nature of the tapestries, especially given the fact that the panels that now hang at the Cloisters in New York were once hung in the sleeping quarters of the duc de La Rochefoucauld, their sixteenth-century owner. His chateau Verteuil is about fifty miles from Albi, which was once the geographical heart of the Albigensian heresy.

The place of legends and folk tales in cultural history has great significance. The key question is not "Where did this story come from?" More important are the questions "Why was this particular story so well-beloved? What chord did it strike with the people of the time? What about this story touched their hearts and minds?" The legend of the unicorn must have touched a special chord with Europeans of the Middle Ages, because it received an *enormous* amount of attention.

The Grail Heresy and the Hunted Unicorn

The story of the unicorn's being ruthlessly hunted and killed may well have represented the "heretical" version of Jesus' life, which included his human masculinity. The image of a married Jesus was anathema to the established Church of Rome. In his analysis of the unicorn tapestries already cited, John Williamson notes that the unicorn was a symbol for male virility. I have concluded that because the unicorn kept appearing in works of art and because it was so popular, the apologists for doctrine tried desperately to give it orthodox and mystical interpretations, deliberately bypassing the physical evidence. Their explanations border on the bizarre. One traditional explanation of the unicorn with his head in the lap of the maiden is that the maiden is the Virgin Mary and the unicorn is Christ seeking to become incarnate in her womb. But that explanation misses the phallic significance of the head of the unicorn, his lifted horn, and the lap of the maiden. The lady in the garden most certainly represents the Goddess of the ancient world, seated in her garden waiting to embrace the Bridegroom/King.

Like the mythical unicorn, who would rather die than be enslaved, the Albigensian heresy of the Grail was ruthlessly hunted. The tapestries displayed at the Cloisters show details of the legend. First the hunters are shown preparing for the hunt. The unicorn in the second panel is kneeling before a stream issuing from a fountain. He is dipping his horn into the water while numerous animals wait to drink from the stream.

This scene has very strong symbolic associations with the heresy, whose itinerate preachers were known as Cathari or "the pure ones." The "waters of truth" flowing from the Catholic Church were believed by the heretics to be polluted through the teaching of false doctrines, especially those concerning the human nature of Jesus. The horn symbolically represents the virility of Jesus, precisely the doctrine that was at the heart of the heresy. So, logically, as far as the heretics were concerned, it was the horn of the unicorn that would purify the polluted doctrine of the church.

John Williamson's marvelous book notes that many of the plants growing near the stream are toxic, reflecting the poisonous waters issuing from the polluted fountain. Significant in this panel of the tapestry, he notes, is the presence of the malevolent "white campion" or "death flower," also known as the "devil's flower" occupying a conspicuous position right between the legs of the central hunter, hinting at his evil intent.

In the third panel of the tapestry, the hunters are trying to prod the unicorn across a stream. And in the fourth, he is defending himself, kicking and ferociously goring one of the hounds. This is odd symbolism for Christ, who is supposed to have gone willingly and docilely to his fate on the cross. But it is an accurate portrayal of the Albigensian Cathars, whose menfolk bravely defended their homeland of Provence against the rapacious mercenaries of the Vatican and the French king for a generation before succumbing to superior force at Montségur.

The fifth panel is unfortunately comprised of two fragments from which a large piece is missing. The unicorn has found his way to the garden, which is surrounded by red and white roses growing along the fence. The woman in the tapestry fragment is the serving woman of the lady of the garden, whose delicate hand (the only part of her that remains) is caressing the neck of the unicorn. The rest of the tapestry, the portion portraying the lady herself, is the only piece missing from any of the seven panels. One must wonder whether this loss was intentional—it often is! In all probability, the lady was holding the mirror universally associated with the love goddess. It is unlikely in my opinion that this part of the tapestry was destroyed accidentally while the rest of the panels were left intact. The unicorn may have had his hooves in her lap, as in the other tapestry series. Or some

other symbol in the panel may have made the identity of the love goddess so obvious that it was deliberately destroyed by a well-meaning
custodian of the orthodox faith, as the tarot trumps portraying The
Papess and The Empress in the Charles VI deck were most probably
destroyed for bearing heretical symbols.

In the sixth tapestry of the hunt series, the unicorn has been brutally sacrificed, his carcass thrown over a horse. The establishment
has hunted and slain the marvelous unicorn; the Christ of the heretics is dead, along with their doctrines, their families, and their hopes
for the Millennium. According to John Williamson's study, the flora
and fauna of this panel reflect the death of the unicorn, defeated and
betrayed, and his journey to the realm of the underworld.

We have already noticed that the language of ecstasy used in the
songs of the troubadours indicted by the Inquisition as heretical in
the thirteenth century was later "laundered" by the church and made
to apply to the Virgin Mary and to Christ, reaching sublime heights
in the writings of the medieval mystics. I am not content with the traditional interpretation of the hunt of the unicorn, culminating with
the death of the mythical one-horned beast in the sixth panel and his
resurrection in the enclosed garden of the seventh. I believe that these
interpretations were an *ex post facto* laundering in an attempt to give
mystical Christian meaning to these significant heretical works of
art. Just as the churches of Christians were erected on shrines of ancient pagan deities and Christian names and legends given to those
former gods and goddesses, so the church has always tried to interpret
the unicorn as orthodox. But no matter how hard they tried to ra-
tionalize, the unicorn was always and remains a particularly exotic
symbol for the virility of the Bridegroom/King.

This theme of fertility and sexuality is underscored by the iconography of the trees in the tapestries. The acorns and pine cones are
visual images of masculinity. The orange tree represents the conjugal
union of the sexes: its leaves, blossoms, and fruit are all present on the
tree at the same time, and its blossoms were traditionally carried by
brides. Traditionally, too, the pomegranate symbolized fecundity,

"bursting with seeds." The holly is feminine, bearing white blossoms and red berries, the colors of passion and purity, the Sister-Bride. But its leaves are evergreen and spiked; they represent the masculine. This Christmas favorite seems to represent the incarnation of both male and female aspects of God. And it is interesting to note that the holly tree is one bush of the botanical garden that needs to be cross-fertilized by a partner in order to bear its brilliant red berries.

I believe that the unicorn in the tapestries represents the virile Jesus of the Grail heresy. His reputation for purifying the waters is understood; that was the claim of the Cathars from the beginning: that their doctrines were purer—that is, closer to the faith of the Apostles—than those of the Roman church. Like the unicorn, their version of the Christian faith was cut down, betrayed, and brutally butchered. But because truth is eternal and cannot be destroyed, in the end the unicorn is resting under the pomegranate tree in the enclosed garden.

The seventh panel, which was not part of the original series, adds a dramatic twist to the story (plate 25). Here the marvelous unicorn is surrounded by the medieval floral symbols of betrothal, fertility, and sexuality—including potent and popular aphrodisiacs![7] The male orchid, conspicuously silhouetted against the white body of the unicorn, is called in French a *testicule de prêtre*, a "priest's testicle." The cuckoopint is an icon for intercourse, while the periwinkle is reputed to engender love between men and women. The bistort aids conception, the dandelion's juice increases the flow of semen, the violet represents lust, and the stock gillyflower symbolizes female fecundity. All these symbolic plants found in the seventh panel are carefully identified in Williamson's work. The red juice staining the white coat of the unicorn comes from the overripe fruit of the pomegranate tree above, ancient symbol for the fecundity of the womb. And prominently situated in the center of the picture is the common iris, the model for the fleur-de-lis or "little sword" of the Merovingians.

In the final panel, the unicorn is resting in the enclosed garden, which is the symbol for the Bride. Like the tenets of the heresy, he is not dead but very much alive. He is taunting the establishment from the seventh panel. They cannot kill the truth or the sacred king; both have a way of surviving the most heinous tortures and being renewed! The unicorn tapestries, owned and cherished as they were by families in the southern regions of France, might easily be interpreted as illustrations of the great unacknowledged heresy of the Middle Ages, the heresy of the physical virility of Jesus and of his role as the sacrificed Bridegroom/King of Israel echoed in Middle Eastern and Celtic myth.

There is another clue from the unicorn tapestries that links them irrevocably with the heresy. We have already itemized the prevalent symbols of the love goddess: the roses, the crescent moon, the bunnies, and the mirror. And both the lion and the unicorn we know to be symbols for Jesus Christ and for the kings of Israel. In the tapestries at the Cluny Museum, the lady has the letter X fashioned into the shoulders of her gown in two of the panels, which might possibly be an accidental matter of fashion. But in the tapestries of the hunt, in the final panel, the letter X occupies a central position and cannot have been made unconsciously.

In this series, the letters A and E are woven into the corners and into the center of virtually all seven panels. These letters have caused a great deal of controversy. A brief glance at Bayley's *Lost Language of Symbolism* may dispel the theory that these initials are those of the nobleman who requested the tapestry or perhaps of his bride-to-be (although that will always remain a distinct possibility). The letter A, formed as it is in the tapestries, is a stylized glyph for *aleph* and *tau*, the alpha and omega of the Hebrew alphabet. It means "the First and the Last." It is both an epithet for the unseen God and a prayer for the peaceful Millennium (containing the letter M in its interior). This sign is prevalent among the watermarks of the Middle Ages. The letter E is also explained in Bayley's volume: it means "the Living God." Perhaps the tapestries were made to honor that Living God, "the Alpha and the Omega," rather than any human patron.

But even more significant than these letters is the cord that attaches them to the pomegranate tree in the seventh panel of the *Hunt of the Unicorn* tapestry. The cord is wrapped around the trunk of the tree so that it forms the letter X in the very center of the tree trunk and of the entire panel. And just to make sure that this X is understood as conscious, it occurs twice! Because the heretics so often used the letter X as a secret code for their faith, it is not at all surprising to find it in the center of the enclosed orchard of pomegranates where the Sacred Marriage is celebrated—the garden of the Sister-Bride.

CHAPTER VIII

THE BRIDE IN FOLKLORE AND LEGEND

We cannot leave the subject of the heresy without mentioning the related and recurrent theme of the lost princess in the folklore of Europe. But first let us review our quest.

We know the Holy Grail was said to be the vessel that once contained the blood of Jesus. We also know that the Grail heresy implied that certain families in southern France could be traced back to Jesus and Mary Magdalen. Whether or not this thesis is true, it had an enormous impact on Western civilization. Connected to this thesis, the ecstatic songs of the troubadours in the twelfth and thirteenth centuries were very likely an outgrowth of the cult of the feminine that was indigenous to Occitania/Provence. The Inquisition branded the songs of the troubadours heretical and demanded that they be changed. Under the vigilant eyes of the inquisitors, the cult of the feminine was channeled into a reverence for the Virgin Mary, and it became ostensibly *her* praises that were sung and her image that was honored in the cathedrals of Europe from the twelfth century on.

During the same century, which saw the return of the Crusaders and the upsurge of heresies we have discussed, the Church of Rome made an all-out attempt to identify "Our Lady," the Domina, with Mary the *mother* of Jesus. A newly proclaimed feast of Mary, the Feast of the Immaculate Conception, was established in 1140 at Lyons in Provence. This feast fostered the misunderstanding that the Virgin Mary was "immaculately" conceived by her parents (Anna and Joachim, according to church tradition), separating her from any suggestion of ordinary humanity. Saint Bernard of Clairvaux, a contemporary of this proclamation, declared that the new feast was one of which "the custom of the church knew nothing and reason did not approve."[1] This misunderstood doctrine of the Virgin Mary "conceived without sin" managed to reflect the prevailing medieval view, fostered by the church, that sex, even within marriage, was somehow sinful. We might stop to ask what our world would look like if we had been taught instead that sex was a sacred, joyful, and meaningful expression of love between partners, as it was in the garden of the Beloved.

It is interesting to note that at the end of the Albigensian Crusade in which the king of France and the pope collaborated to lay waste the entire southern portion of what is now France, the surviving daughters of the nobles of that region were deliberately wed to scions of the northern French families—who were not, one presumes, tainted with the heresy. I have speculated that this was an attempt to dissipate the bloodline of the Vine. The records of the Inquisition avoided mention of this aspect of its campaign against the southern heretics, preferring to dwell on the "doctrines" and practices of the Cathar believers and later the Templars as the reason for their persecution. But as most modern scholars agree, the Albigensian heretics, who adhered to several different sects and persuasions, practiced a living and charismatic version of the Christian faith. Saint Bernard of Clairvaux said of the Cathars of his day that no sermons were more thoroughly Christian than theirs and that their morals were pure.[2] And yet they were systematically wiped out by French and Papal mercenaries, abetted by the Inquisition officially formed for that purpose.

The faith of the heretics has been obscured because of the incredible violence with which it was persecuted by authorities of orthodoxy. But, as we are learning, the adherents of the Grail heresy left a legacy in art and song that cannot be ignored. The folk have a way of knowing with the heart. And the faith of the heretics was woven into their stories in numerous versions, some of which we can mention here.

The legends of the Grail were written as poems in the twelfth and thirteenth centuries and circulated widely in the courts of Europe.

Those same courts received the troubadours as guests and eventually, in the fifteenth century, were introduced to games played with the enigmatic tarot cards. One might say there was an underground networking going on, keeping the tenets of the Albigensian faith just under the surface so that the Inquisition could not reach them.

One clear evidence of this is the watermarks found in the paper on which the Bible and other such popular books as *The Romance of the Rose* and *The Song of Roland* were printed. Even these widely popular works have particular significance. The passages of *The Romance of the Rose* written by Jean le Meun are an alchemical treatise. And Roland, Charlemagne's nephew, was the most popular of all French heroes in literature. It was Roland's horn, "Oliphant," pictured among the Albigensian watermarks, that was the symbol for heretical preaching because its blast could split rock. Other traces of the heresy include the hidden messages found in the religious art of Europe, which we have already examined. The adherents of the heresy were very resourceful!

The Black Bride

One of the flowing streams that carried the heresy through the centuries was the body of tales we call folklore. One of the most popular of these was "Cinderella." There are two very significant facts about Cinderella that are relevant to our search: she was a "lost feminine," scorned and kept in "exile" and obscurity, relegated to the kitchen; and her face, as her name suggests, was covered with soot. She was, in fact, an echo of the Black Madonna image mentioned earlier. The "dark" or "sooty-faced" serving girl recalls the swarthy bride of Solomon, sunburned from her labor in her brothers' vineyards (Cant. 1:6). It also recalls Sarah, the dark-skinned child on the boat with Mary Magdalen and her kin. Cinderella is called "Aschenputtel" in German, another echo of the verses in the Book of Lamentations mourning the fate of Jerusalem and the "Daughter of Sion": "Those brought up in purple now cling to the ash heaps" (Lam. 4:4). The lost "sooty-faced" princess Cinderella is finally able, with the help of the little mice and birds (the elements of nature come to aid her!), to fulfill her destiny as bride of the bachelor prince, and everyone in their realm lives happily ever after. Marriage invariably heals the wasteland in the fairy tales of Europe.

Modern feminists have turned this tale upside down. Despising the insinuation that the woman must be fulfilled by a man, they miss the point of the story: that it is the *prince* who is passionately seeking *his* lost counterpart.

The motif of the "blackness" of the lost princess mentioned in earlier chapters—and her identity as the dark Sister-Bride and the Daughter of Sion—is too important to pass over without pausing. It is reflected in the shrines of the Black Madonna in Europe, some of which contain statues of great antiquity.[3] *Our Lady of Rocamadour*, a statue near Toulouse in the heart of the Albigensian region, is believed to have been visited by Charlemagne in the ninth century, and *Our Lady of Oropa* in the Biellese Alps in Switzerland is thought to be of fifth-century origin. The latter is made of cedar, with its face and hands deliberately painted jet black. Other statues include *Our Lady of Valcourt* (tenth century), *Our Lady of Myans*, patroness of Savoy (a pre–twelfth-century cedar carving), *Our Lady of Montserrat* (twelfth century), *Our Lady of LaSarte* (thirteenth century), and *Notre Dame under the Earth* in the crypt of the Cathedral of Chartres. All of these statues of the Black Madonna seem to predate the power of the Inquisition.

A second popular statue of the Black Madonna is located at Chartres. Recalling our discussion of Boaz, the broken left pillar of the Temple of Solomon in Jerusalem, it seems more than coincidental this other Black Madonna at Chartres is called *Our Lady of the Pillar*. Of course, the obvious reason is that she stands upon a pillar. But someone must have chosen this particular pose for her. Can it be another cryptic reference to the other Mary, the widow of Jesus?

One of the most famous of the Black Madonnas is the icon of *Our Lady of Czestochowa*, the patroness of Poland to whom Pope John Paul II has a special devotion. She is said to have preserved the Polish nation from destruction by the armies of Gustavus Adolphus during the Thirty Years War (1618–1648). Perhaps a later generation will credit her with the freeing of Eastern Europe from Soviet domination and communism! Legend says that this icon of Our Lady was brought to Poland from Byzantium in the tenth century. Curiously, the right cheek of this Madonna bears an ugly gash. She is not only dark; she is wounded.

Two pertinent Scripture passages help to explain the wounded cheek of the Black Madonna. One is from the fourth chapter of Micah, only a few verses after the reference to the Magdal-eder, the "stronghold of the daughter of Sion," through whom dominion (of the House of David) will one day be restored (Mic. 4:8–10). It says, "With a rod they strike on the cheek the ruler of Israel" (Mic. 4:14b). This scripture is often applied to Jesus, who was avowedly tortured by Roman soldiers—struck and scourged and crowned with thorns. The suffering servant of Isaiah 53, understood by Christians to be the prototype of Jesus, and the Black Madonna of Czestochowa are a matching pair. The symbolic "blackness" of the suffering servant in Isaiah 53 was noted and elaborated by Saint Bernard of Clairvaux in his twelfth-century commentary on the Song of Songs.[4]

A famous painting, Road to Calvary (plate 28) by the Italian painter Simone Martini (1284–1344), depicts Mary Magdalen with a similar slash on her right cheek. In the painting, Mary Magdalen and Jesus are both wearing rose-colored gowns, again a matching pair. In the painting, the X of the cross that Jesus carries frames the torso and distraught, scarred face of Mary Magdalen, who is disproportionately large—as if she, not Jesus, were the central figure in the scene. The theme of the abused feminine, it seems, is not just casually represented by this other Mary. There is little chance that the X in this picture is an accidental use of the esoteric symbol of the heretics.

The second Scripture reference of which we are reminded by the Black Madonna's wound is found in the Song of Songs. The Bride speaks of her search for her lover who has departed: "The watchmen came upon me as they made their rounds; they struck me and wounded me . . . the guardians of the walls" (Cant. 5:7). Clearly the "guardians of the walls" are the custodians of the establishment who do not wish to allow the feminine, the Bride, to be united with her Beloved and given status as an equal partner.

This archetypal theme of the separated lovers and their quest for one another probably occurs in every language and lore on Earth. In the twelfth century a curious legend was told of a dark Middle Eastern bride who sought her Crusader husband, from whom she had accidentally become separated, all the way from her homeland to the city of London. The story was said to have been that of the father of the popular martyred English saint-hero Thomas à Becket, whose conflict with King Henry II is well documented.

The twentieth-century storyteller Thomas B. Costain wrote a novel based on this legend. The dark bride's name was Miriam, and she had a child with her. For years her search was obstructed by greedy merchants, devious sailors, illness, and deprivation before she was finally reunited with her English husband. She was of Middle Eastern blood and the novel is called *The Black Rose*. The hero, Walter of Gurney, was a young nobleman who brought back from his journey to China (of all things!) the secret of papermaking, the common craft of the Albigensian heretics. The romantic theme of the separated lovers culminates in their reunion: the wasteland is healed. Is it only coincidental that Thomas Costain also wrote an eloquent novel entitled *The Silver Chalice*, about the lost cup from which Jesus drank at the Last Supper? Perhaps Thomas Costain was also a Freemason—or perhaps he was just magnificently intuitive! Our fascination with the lost princess and the Grail has not been diminished through the centuries.

European Fairy Tales

"Cinderella" embodies the belief that when the Bride is found and restored to the bachelor prince, the realm will be healed. This motif plays over and over in our fairy tales. The essential theme is the quest for the true counterpart of the prince. Another variation occurs in the tale of Briar Rose, often called "Sleeping Beauty" in English versions. In this story, Princess Briar Rose is pricked by a poisoned spindle and sent to sleep for a hundred (some say a thousand) years. Finally the prince has to hack his way through the hedge of briars that has grown up around the Beloved, hiding her very existence. Only sheer determination on the part of the prince unites this pair. The image of the impetuous prince slashing his way through the thicket of thorn bushes in an attempt to find his lost princess, his "other half," is particularly significant for our modern world. The wounded male recklessly brandishing his sword is not only hurt and frustrated, he is also dangerous. The sooner he is united with his own lost, scorned, and repudiated feminine side, the better!

In still another familiar story, the princess Snow White is ordered murdered by her evil stepmother. There is almost always a malicious, jealous step-mother or an ugly old witch trying to keep the prince separated from his counterpart; she is trying to keep the Bride from replacing *herself*. This wicked mother sees the beautiful princess in her magic mirror and tempts the maiden with a shiny apple, which poisons her. Only the timely arrival of the prince saves Snow White from the dire consequences of the deadly apple.

Yet another favorite fairy tale that contains rich associations with the theme of the Lost Bride of Jesus is "Rapunzel." This time the maiden is imprisoned in a tower by a wicked witch who has taken her from her father. Rapunzel is famous for her extravagant hair and her beautiful voice, "the voice of the Bride" (Jer. 33:11a) so often mentioned in folklore. A passing prince hears her singing and manages to persuade her to let down her golden braids so that he can climb up to visit her in her prison tower. Here the clues that tantalize us are the hair of the lady and the tower, for these same symbols are prominent in the lore of the Mary called Magdalen, who dried the feet of Jesus with her hair and whose epithet means "tower" in Hebrew.

These symbols are also present in the strange stories surrounding Saint Barbara, a classic example of the way symbols and identities of saints and folktale characters are commingled. Saint Barbara, according to legends that the church now calls spurious, was a virgin martyr, the daughter of a pagan gentleman of the third century in Syria. She wanted to be a Christian, and her father, horrified by that prospect, locked her up in a tower. The priest who came secretly to instruct her in the faith is said to have climbed her braids to enter her prison. Wild as this story's claims appear to us, Saint Barbara was not discredited until the new calendar of the Roman Catholic Church was published in 1969! For centuries she was depicted in Christian iconography—a beautiful lady with fabulous long hair carrying her tower in her arms.

But Saint Barbara's case has another interesting feature that I believe is relevant. Her name means "foreigner," from the same root as "barbarian" (*barber* means "bearded"), which in classical times designated anyone who did not speak Greek. In some versions of the Cinderella story, the little lost princess is called "Barbarella" because she comes from a far country. She is an unknown and unrecognized "foreigner" in exile. In one version of the Cinderella story, she says, "I am a princess from a faraway land. You do not know me." Perhaps we do!

Recalling that the word *magdala* in Hebrew means "tower" (with connotations also of "stronghold" or "fortress"), I am inclined to believe that the foreigner with the marvelous hair and the tower in her arms in medieval iconography is really the Magdalen. In the Song of Songs, the Sister-Bride says of herself, "I am a wall and my breasts are like towers" (Cant. 8:10). She is referring to herself as a "walled city," that is, Sion. The dark Bride—and the tower and glorious long hair that are her symbols—preceded the stories that were made up about Saint Barbara to explain them. She is surely the Sister-Bride of Canticles and the Magdal-eder of Micah—Mary, the exiled daughter of Sion.

This intuitive leap is confirmed by a curious practice found in the celebration of Saint Barbara's Day in central Europe. On her feast day, the fourth of December, when there is snow on the ground and the trees are bare of leaves, the dwellers of a mountain village in Silesia go out to gather barren boughs and bring them into their homes, where they put them in water. Here the branches burst into bloom in honor of the Lady of the Tower! This seems to me to be a folk remembrance of the miraculous flowering of the staff of Jesse, the barren branch of the kings of Judah, through the motherhood of the Magdal-eder. She is not the fairy-tale bride Rapunzel, nor is she Saint Barbara. She is Mary Magdalen, the foreign princess from across the sea whose distinguishing feature in every medieval painting is the glorious hair that she once used to wipe her tears from the feet of Christ.

As if we needed additional confirmation of this confusion of Saint Barbara with the Magdalen, it is enough to note that she is the patron saint of fortifications. The list of professionals who call Saint Barbara their patron includes architects, stonemasons, and military engineers and artillerymen who build and defend fortifications, the "walled cities" and castles of medieval history. (Remember the chivalric order of warrior-builders—the Templars?) To this day, the colors of the United States Army Corps of Engineers are red and white, their insignia is the castle with two towers, and the Artillery Ball is held to celebrate Saint Barbara's feast day, the fourth of December, at United States military bases around the globe.

I do not here intend to recount all our childhood fairy tales. My purpose is only to show the prevalence of the theme of the wounded, lost, or imprisoned feminine counterpart of the handsome prince. The earliest known versions of the Cinderella story in Europe date from about the ninth century. This was the very period when the Merovingian kings had been deposed and supplanted, their heritage usurped and obliterated by the Carolingian heirs of Pepin in alleged collusion with the Vatican. Perhaps the "stepmother" who tried so often to destroy the little princess deserved her evil reputation.

The Cauldron

Old legends of the Celtic people (Ireland, Wales, Scotland, and France) contain references to a magic cup or cauldron. This vessel was symbolic of the feminine. It provided food and blessing in abundance, similar to the "horn of plenty," which is also associated with the horn or "trumpet" of the Word of God—the magical horn whose "wake-up call" will cause the desert to bloom. Both the Grail and the magical horn of medieval legend take on this property of bringing eternal well-being, peace, and prosperity to the land and its people.

The Sangraal of early French legend easily became confused with the cauldron of Bran in the Welsh bardic tradition. During the Crusades, the men of Christian Europe sat at their campfires listening to the tales of their bards and minstrels, and their favorite motifs were swapped and interwoven. Gradually the feminine connotations of the chalice and the cauldron were obscured, but these folktales retained the image of the lost princess even after the association with the Grail was lost. Later poets copied the themes of the Arthurian cycle and elaborated upon them without knowing the tenets of the heresy. The point of the story was lost and then newly articulated in the retelling, in much the same way that the tarot cards painted by later copyists lost many of the specific Grail symbols that had originally identified them with the heresy. Instead of being an Albigensian catechism, the cards became a reservoir of a more general occult wisdom and universal esoteric symbolism. And, as in the case of the fairy tales and legends of Europe, the specific references were gradually forgotten under the vigilant scrutiny of the Inquisition, which would not allow them to be spoken aloud.

Attempts to Restore the Feminine

The twelfth-century attempt to restore the forgotten Bride of Jesus was thwarted by orthodoxy. Yet the cult of the woman praised in the songs of the troubadours contained the seeds of a whole new value system that was struggling to take root in Europe. This value system put new emphasis on the Gospel teachings of equality and fraternity along with a new emphasis on the world, the flesh, and the feminine. The motifs of the *Carmina Burana*, the songs of the vagabond poets whose motto was *carpe diem*, "seize the day," blossomed and flourished. Wandering students and entertainers carried the message of Eros/relationship from place to place, planting seeds that later cracked the walls of the establishment. The later movements of the Reformation were sparked by this earlier attempt to break the chains of tyranny.

One of the legacies of the early movement was the Protestant repudiation of celibacy (and sometimes even masculinity) as a prerequisite for Christian ministry. Even today, the rising feminine conscious-ness survives in our understanding of the political left, which tradi-tionally concerns itself with the needs of the *anawim*, the "little ones" of Hebrew scripture.

Overall, however, as we have noted, orthodox Christianity forced the cult of woman to be channeled into the cult of the Virgin Mary. The Mother and Sister aspects of the feminine were honored, but the Bride aspect was sublimated. The church could not accept the flesh-and-blood wife of Jesus. The only bride of Christ who was acceptable to the hierarchy was the church itself—the entire community of be-lievers—or its microcosm, the individual soul. The passionate lan-guage of courtly poetry and the marriage imagery of the Garden were adopted by the mystics of the late Middle Ages. And the relationship with Jesus, the eternal and mystical Bridegroom of the soul, was indi-vidualized as the doctrine of the feminine was rearticulated by the church. Only a mystical marriage of Jesus was allowed.

In many paintings of the Assumption and Coronation of Our Lady, the Virgin Mary, the Mother of Jesus, is extolled as Bride. In these paintings, she is sometimes pictured seated at the left hand of God, opposite Jesus. Here she is the acknowledged "mother of all," model of Holy Mother Church. In this sense the Virgin Mary provided a strong feminine presence for the Catholic Church, but always at the discretion of the male hierarchy. In raising the mother of Jesus to be Queen of Heaven in the celestial paradigm, at least one beautiful im-age of the eternal feminine principle was preserved, although the flesh-and-blood wife of Jesus was deliberately denied.

But in spite of all the denial, the folk never forgot the exiled woman-child at the hearth, sooty faced and abused, waiting for the fulfillment of her destiny: her eventual marriage to the bachelor prince.

THE DESERT SHALL BLOOM

The legend promises that the restored Grail will have the power to heal the wasteland. When it is returned to the crippled Fisher King, it will heal his woundedness, the source of the desolation that plagues his realm. And the Grail, we suggest, is the lost feminine— the Sister-Bride of Christianity, the wife of Jesus. What would our world have been like if the Bride in Christianity had never been lost? And what will it be like when she is restored?

The imbalance of our fundamental institutions reflecting a father God at the peak of an all-male trinity, $\triangle$, has had a devastating influence on the Western world. With the accelerated pace of events due to scientific advances in the last three hundred years, and especially in the last fifty, the fracture in Western society and in the human psyche has become more and more apparent. The pollution of our planet Earth and the flagrant abuse of her children are closely related to this fundamental flaw.

If the Bride had not been lost, the feminine might have been established from the beginning as an equal partner of the male deity. Feminine preferences and attributes would have been honored equally through the centuries, and the resulting integration in the psyche of individuals would have spread to their families and communities. The denial of the feminine as partner and friend has robbed us of ecstasy and reduced our male-female relationships to a distorted shadow of the joy shared by the archetypal couple in the Garden. The wounded male, often overindulged and deeply frustrated, seeks his lost ecstasy in all the wrong places—violence, power, materialism, and the hedonistic pursuit of pleasure—not understanding that it is to be found only in relationship with the feminine.

One of the saddest realities in our culture is that the ascendancy of the wounded masculine has led to emotional exhaustion. Where the feminine is not valued, a man has no real intimacy with his counterpart, his "other half." He often cannot channel his energies into a loving relationship, since his partner is not considered worthy. Deprived of his equal opposite because the feminine is viewed as an inferior object, the frustrated ascendant male causes burnout: "where the sun always shines, there's a desert below." Forests wither, streams dry up, the earth cracks. The wasteland ensues.

The Paradigm for Wholeness

The Holy Grail, the Lost Bride of Jesus, is the missing piece of an ancient paradigm for wholeness. Long forgotten in Western civilization, there was a mandala honored in the oldest cultures of the world. It was based on the archetypal symbols of male and female, the masculine "blade" and the feminine "chalice" or Grail. This holy mandala is the symbol for the Sacred Marriage. Significantly, this very same symbol is found in the esoteric writings of the medieval master alchemists, where it was equated with the "philosopher's stone" of spiritual transformation.[1] The forgotten model of the Sacred Marriage of male and female, heaven and earth, is still a mandala for harmony, wholeness, and partnership.

In the Neolithic period, according to recent scholarship, there was a golden age when differences between male and female did not involve a power struggle for control. Instead, relationships were based on partnerships in which the gifts of each were accepted and appreciated. This time in prehistory, once believed to be mythical, can now be reconstructed from artifacts found in sites of Neolithic civilizations that worshiped a gracious and bountiful Mother Goddess. Findings of archaeology testify to societies in which the gifts of women—nurturing, cherishing, and educating the young—were honored, where the "blade" was used to till the soil rather than to intimidate, where life was held sacred, where arts and crafts flourished and creativity was cause for celebration.

Fascinating research concerning these ancient mother-oriented cultures and societies worldwide has been collected by Merlin Stone, Marija Gimbutas, and Riane Eisler, to name only a few. Recent discoveries reveal the fact that in numerous Paleolithic and Neolithic shrines dating from 7000–3500 B.C., the letter V is associated with the Mother Goddess.[2] The conclusion of Marija Gimbutas, a cultural anthropologist who encountered this ideogram in the shrines of Old Europe (an area including Turkey, the Balkans, and the Ukraine), is that it was used in Old European script and may have been a representation of the Goddess manifested as a bird.[3]

The study of archaic symbolism leads me to question the conclusion that the V represents a bird. The V is in fact the archaic symbol for the "vessel" or "womb" of all life. It is the archetypal chalice. And it is symbolic of the Earth itself, the only life-bearing planet we know.

I would like to suggest here that the archetypal symbols for male and female, the ∧ and ∨, depict an ancient dualism that can be reconciled and used to form the age-old paradigm for wholeness. This visual image is logically the hexagram, the ✡. The Sacred Marriage of the Hindu god Shiva and his counterpart, Shakti, in the ancient lore of India is portrayed with this geometric design.[4] From their sacred Cosmic Dance of the Opposites, which symbolizes the interplay of the positive and negative forces of energy, harmony spreads into all aspects of the life of people. This harmony is reflected in the well-being of the community and in the fertility of its crops and herds. The hexagram seems to have spread westward from India to the Middle East and Europe.

While the word carries other connotations, I wish to use the term *Eros* to represent the feminine principle of love and relatedness in the Jungian sense, yoking it with its companion masculine principle of Logos/reason, which is associated with power and light. These two principles are called yin/yang in Oriental philosophy. The neglected principle of Eros/relatedness, represented by the V of the Great Goddess, has been devalued over the centuries since those far-off millennia when it was so highly revered and deeply cherished. Occasionally, appreciation for the feminine has surfaced and then been repressed. We have examined evidence of the brief flowering of the "red rose," the Bride, in the twelfth century in Provence, before its being forced underground by the Inquisition.

Our worship of an exclusively male image of God is both distorted and dangerous. According to the principle "As in Heaven, so on Earth," male preferences and male domination cause society to form institutions based on a Δ "male" model, with power concentrated at the top and the exploited masses imprisoned at the bottom. This is the model for dictatorship and oppression. In a society where the feminine is given equal time, children are nurtured and widows are consoled; arts, letters, music and dance are encouraged; childhood is joyful; work is productive; and people live in harmony.

It is interesting to note that after millennia of wars and the scourges of plague and famine that accompany them, the Mediterranean lands of the Greek and Roman empires during the centuries directly preceding the birth of Jesus had developed a widespread cult of Isis, "Queen of Heaven and Earth." Marie-Louise von Franz, a student and interpreter of the works of the psychologist Carl Jung, attributes this cult of the Goddess to the fact that the masculine mode of consciousness gets tired.[5] In effect, it finally suffers burnout from its own excessive concentration on mental or "Logos" achievement. It eventually needs respite from its frantic goal- and destination-oriented activity. It seeks rest and refuge in the feminine, the shade, and the night.

In her book *Alchemy*, Marie-Louise von Franz notes that at the end of a patriarchal civilization there comes an "enantiodromia"—the power of the "burned-out" male principle is handed over to a "goddess" and then later reasserts itself in the new era, which subsequently institutionalizes new ideas and a new cultural direction. The worn-out images of the old ways are laid aside, and new archetypes are found to carry the message.

This phenomenon was illustrated in the life of the early Christian church when the patriarchs took the "good news" of Jesus preached in the streets and institutionalized it with rules, rituals, and written treatises.[6] The feminine principle of relatedness had been the early practice of the Christian communities, where a oneness in the Spirit had dissolved class and sex barriers, allowing women and slaves to participate fully in the life of the group—even permitting them to preach and to prophesy. The freedom and equality afforded to women, slaves, and foreigners by the Christian message was, within a hundred years of its inception, already being rethought by the men in charge, and new guidelines for ethical behavior and religious practice were being formulated. The era of partnership had been short lived, superseded by a return to the dominant male role and the relative subordination of women in the church and in society at large.

The hierarchical model Δ of patriarchal institutions, where all decisions and power rest with the autocratic ruler or oligarchy at the top, is losing its vitality in the wake of the powerful feminine consciousness being expressed in our modern world. These institutions, which teach that strict obedience is the highest of all virtues, begin to crumble under the "feminine" influence of free thinking, creativity, intuition, and relatedness. This resurrection of the feminine has allowed the things that women traditionally care most about—the education and nurturing of children and the enhancement of the quality of life—gradually to become visible on the agenda. Under the influence of this resurgent feminine principle, there is hope that the peoples of Earth may yet become enlightened, cherishing the unique gift of life of which this "water-carrying" planet Earth is custodian. The "voice of the bride" (Jer. 33:11a) is being heard at last.

The sign that Winston Churchill first flashed as a symbol of the determination of the Allies to win victory in World War II was the letter V. By some quirk of the unconscious, this symbol has since become the universal sign of democratic movements around the globe. Consciously or unconsciously, the V "chalice" is an invocation of the Goddess. It represents the feminine principle of Eros/relatedness. But the V cannot stand alone. A society based on the ▽ model will surely topple! It still needs and will always need the counterbalance of Logos/reason, which is manifested in law, order, discipline and self-restraint, in order to produce the life-giving equilibrium of the ✡.

The leaders of patriarchal societies, the "guardians of the walls" (Cant. 5:7), do not understand their own woundedness in denying their feminine counterpart as they struggle to protect their power and the status quo. An interesting story is told of Saint Thomas Aquinas (1225–1274), the great articulator and definer of Catholic doctrine and one of the principal architects of the walls of the present establishment.[7] Saint Thomas is the patron saint of sudden death. It seems that shortly before he died, this scholarly priest found himself unable to continue writing his *Summa Theologica* and declared that all his writings were like straw! He was on a trip a short time later when he hit his head sharply on the branch of a tree and was knocked off his donkey. That evening, feeling shaken and ill, he stayed the night in a monastery in the Austrian Alps. The monks persuaded him to leave his bed in order to give them the benefit of his wisdom, and he did not deny them. The topic he chose for his talk was the Song of Songs, and while he was offering an interpretation of the lines "Come my beloved, let us go forth into the field" (Cant. 7:12), he suddenly died.

The scripture that this saint felt most precious was the subject of his final discourse, the canticle of the Sacred Marriage! What a shame that this revealing episode is forgotten, while the *Summa Theologica* is still taught in seminaries around the world—even though it was repudiated centuries ago by its own author! The "guardians of the walls," obsessed with maintaining order and control, have managed through the centuries to keep the Bride from becoming an equal partner. The devaluing of the feminine must be reversed, not at the expense of the masculine but as its long-desired counterpart, the Lost Sister-Bride. Together they must go into the fields to till, to sow, and to harvest.

There is an ancient promise found in the Psalms of the Hebrew Bible: "Those that sow in tears shall reap rejoicing . . . and they shall come back rejoicing, carrying their sheaves" (Ps. 126:5–6). This passage prophesies the return of the remnant of Israel from exile in Babylon. It is time again to leave "Babylon," symbolic of the sun- and power-worshiping empire, and to return to the Promised Land "flowing with milk and honey," where the masculine and feminine principles are honored together in partnership and where the ✡ is the blueprint for wholeness.

The male Logos has been enthroned at the right hand of God for centuries, worshiped and glorified in Christian prayers and consciousness, raising Western civilization to "right-handedness." It is time to reclaim Eros, the bridal aspect of divinity. We have known the Logos of God—the Word made flesh in Jesus. Now we must spend time with the Lady of the Garden, basking in her gentleness, her tenderness, her concern and compassion for the *anawim*. These little ones, the "raisins of God," have been scorched and dried under the relentless rays of the ascendant masculine principle.

The Signs of the Dawning Age

Gradually becoming visible, we are told, is the constellation Aquarius, the Water Carrier, which will soon replace Pisces, the Fishes, as the star sign of the age. The sign of Aquarius is two parallel lines of waves, ≈. The meaning of this sign is "the dissolution of forms," but it does not represent water, as one might expect. Astrologers tell us that Aquarius is an "air sign." The forms that may be dissolving under its influence are our patriarchal institutions of government, church, and even family. And the waves that are dissolving them are the figurative waters of the Holy Spirit, the Spirit of Truth. This truth is on the airwaves, the waves of mass communication and the free press, which have made our globe into a village. They are rapidly bringing down the artificial barriers of nation, race, and creed, allowing individuals to see themselves as one flesh with all creation. The space flights of recent decades have enabled us to see "from a distance" our whole planet as it really is, with no fences, no walls. The truth is marching on!

The adherents of the Grail heresy believed that the restoration

and cherishing of the feminine were key to the fulfillment of the millennial promises of universal peace and justice. Perhaps they also hoped
that the time of deliverance would occur in the future dawn of
Aquarius, when the waves of the Water Carrier would dissolve the patriarchal structures of society and a new cultural thrust would occur.
The esoterics and artists of the Middle Ages were steeped in astrology. Their studies in science, philosophy, medicine, and astronomy
led them to form secret societies and to couch their writings in symbols so that they could practice their occult arts in relative safety. A
good example of this is found in the texts of medieval and Renaissance alchemists, who used astrological symbols to explain their discoveries in the fields of philosophy and psychology.

As previously stated, alchemy was not primarily the search for a
metallurgic formula to turn lead into gold. The primary texts of the
old master alchemists refer to the transmutation of a natural person
into a spiritual person. These texts refer us to the Gospel tenets of
service and sacrifice. The crucible is life itself, and the goal is union
with God. The transformed person is one who finds the "philosopher's
stone," often equated with wisdom, or the "pearl of great price." In
some alchemical texts, this wisdom is illustrated with the symbol ✡.
(The dot above the right point represents the presence of God).[8] Here
again we find the sacred "union of opposites" and holiness/wholeness
illustrated by the hexagram.

The symbols of the alchemists are the same as those found among
the Albigensian watermarks, the Rosicrucians, the Freemasons, and
the esoteric artists discussed in earlier chapters. Many of these symbols are being revived in this century by students of medieval civilization and by astrologers. But many of these people seem to have missed
the vital connecting link: the heresy of the Grail and its secret of the
Lost Bride.

Jewish rabbinical tradition teaches that the Ark of the Covenant
kept in the Holy of Holies of Solomon's Temple on Mount Sion contained not only the tablets on which the Ten Commandments were
inscribed, but also a "man and a woman locked in intimacy in the

form of a hexagram."[9] This tradition articulates the fundamental basis of Hebrew society; the tablets represent the precepts of the covenant, and the hexagram symbolizes the *hieros gamos*, the intimate union of the opposites. The meaning of the hexagram is summed up in the Hebrew word *shalom*, meaning "peace and well-being." It is still the prayer of the universe.

Recent research about the feminine aspect of God in the Hebrew tradition reveals that the Holy of Holies was the marriage chamber where the union of Yahweh, the unseen Holy One, with his feminine counterpart, the Shekinah, was consummated.[10] With the destruction of the Temple, so goes the Jewish myth, the relationship of Yahweh and Shekinah (or Matronit, as she was often called) was ruptured, and Yahweh returned to the heavens to reign alone. Meanwhile his bride roamed the earth in exile, like the community of Israel in Diaspora[11]— and like the Magdal-eder and Cinderella!

We find this Sister-Bride, still searching for her lost Bridegroom, in the Song of Songs: "I am black but beautiful as the tents of Cedar" (Cant. 1:5). The bride goes on to explain that the darkness of her skin is a swarthiness from laboring in her brothers' vineyards in the heat of the sun. She is sunburned, swarthy from serving the sun principle. As we have noted, the Song of Songs was understood to have been a wedding song. It was retained among the holy Scriptures of Israel, loved and revered by later generations, and borrowed from Judaism into Christianity. Up until the thirteenth century, the bride was often associated with Mary Magdalen. And the sacred ✡ remained in the rabbinical tradition as the preeminent symbol for the Sacred Marriage, a promise of harmony and well-being.

In many of the myths of the wounded or crippled king or god, including the Fisher King Anfortas in the *Parsifal* poem, the wound is to the foot or thigh—a universal metaphor for the genitals in Western art and literature. The wound of the crippled king is healed only when his feminine counterpart is found. This reunion is the source of the blessing, joy, and fertility that emanates from the nuptial chamber and spreads to the surrounding family and community. Separated partners are healed by their reunion, since their separation in fact constitutes their woundedness!

The Blueprint for the Temple

"Is there anyone who remembers the former glory of this house?" asks the Hebrew prophet Haggai. The date is 520 B.C., and the Temple of Solomon on Mount Sion lies in ruins. The Jews have returned to Israel after their seventy years of exile in Babylon, the city equated with pagan sun worship. The Word of God to Haggai is that the Temple is to be rebuilt and that blessing will begin to flow again when the foundation of the Temple has been laid—not *after* the Temple is finished, but when it is *begun*! When we understand the blueprint of the true Temple—the sacred, life-giving balance of male and female energies inherent in the cosmos itself and the symbolism that portrays the composite wisdom of antiquity—blessing will begin to flow like a gentle river into the parched lands of Earth. As found in the promise of Isaiah, the desert shall bloom. Universal peace and well-being can be restored when the blueprint for the Temple is embraced in our consciousness. The blueprint is the ✡.

An interesting tenet of esoteric wisdom is that the symbol of the cultural thrust of any new age is embryonic and present "at the scene" just as the prior age is dying away. On the night when Jesus was arrested in the Garden of Gethsemane and brought to the Fortress Antonio for questioning, the Gospels report that he was tortured by the Roman soldiers garrisoned there and crowned with thorns. Carved into the flagstones of the Fortress Antonio, in the very hall where Jesus is said to have been scourged, is the emblem of the Sacred Marriage with a dove hovering above it, wings outstretched.[12] The emblem is thought to have been carved there by Roman soldiers of the garrison, perhaps in connection with a popular game like checkers or hopscotch. For whatever reason it was carved in the stone, it seems more than a coincidence that this symbol was present at the scene. This emblem was the sign of the age to come, the age of partnership and wholeness, embryonic in the teachings of Jesus recorded in the Gospels.

The alchemists are known to have used this same sign to denote their philosopher's stone, the goal of their work of transformation. They were probably unaware that the sign appears in the floor of the room where the Bridegroom/King of Israel is said to have been tortured. More likely, their knowledge of geometry and sacred symbol led them to adopt the hexagram because of its intrinsic meaning of wholeness and partnership. This symbol of the ✡ sums up the opening words of the Hebrew Bible found in Genesis 1: "In the beginning God created the heaven and the earth . . . and the spirit of God brooded over the waters." The presence of God, which in the shorthand of the alchemists is a small dot, is represented by the dove in the emblem on the floor of the Fortress Antonio.

In the texts of the alchemists, the star by itself can mean "chaos," while the addition of the dot or the dove renders the meaning "cosmos." The idea here is that the presence and guidance of the Holy Spirit give direction and meaning to the created universe, a teleological worldview deeply rooted in the Judeo-Christian tradition. The dove of the Spirit hovering over the ✡ of the *hieros gamos* found carved in stone in the Fortress Antonio is a symbol of wholeness and spiritual transformation for *all* ages.

It is perhaps relevant that the medieval adherents of the secret doctrines chose not to honor the crucifix. Instead, they regarded it as an instrument of torture, not worthy of veneration. They honored instead the X of enlightenment, the ⋀—promise of the Millennium—and the dove of the Spirit.

The Dove, the Lamb, and the Fish

The dove is one of the most familiar and best loved of all Christian symbols, understood as a sign of the Holy Spirit. The Holy Spirit did not become masculine until it was translated into the Latin *spiritus sanctus*. The Hebrew word used for the Spirit is feminine. In the ancient cosmologies, the Spirit was always feminine, and the dove was the bird that represented this feminine principle. We need to examine this dove, along with two ancient symbols for Jesus, the fish and the lamb. These symbols keep recurring in Christian iconography and they have particular significance to our story of the Lost Bride.

At John's baptism of Jesus in the River Jordan, the sky opened up, and the onlookers must have been surprised to see a dove descending on Jesus. Clearly this dove had symbolic meaning. Doves in the ancient world were sacred to the Goddess—to Aphrodite, Venus, Isis, and Sophia. There has been speculation that this sign in the Gospel narrative was intended to indicate that Jesus was an incarnation or "child" of Sophia, Holy Wisdom, a position commonly held among Gnostic sects in the early centuries of Christianity.

When the Pharisees begged Jesus to give them a sign, he told them that the only sign he would give them was the sign of Jonah (Matt. 16:4). In the wake of the current furor over which of the recorded words of Jesus were actually spoken by Jesus and which were later added by ardent disciples, interpreters, and apologists, perhaps we should look a second time at this "sign of Jonah." The quotation may have been interpreted after the Resurrection to be a prophecy of three days in the tomb, prefigured by the three days that the prophet Jonah is said to have been incarcerated in the belly of the whale. But there is another possible interpretation. In Hebrew, Jonah means "dove."[13] What if Jesus really did say that the sign he would give was the sign of Jonah, and what if this statement was remembered by the community but misunderstood and later embellished? Perhaps what Jesus tried to say was that he had come in the sign of the dove. Surely his disciples already knew that, since Mark's Gospel states that the Spirit in the form of a dove descended upon Jesus at his baptism (Mark 1:10).

The Dawning Age of Pisces

One could thus claim that the charismatic healer and teacher, whose baptismal sign was a dove, was slain as a lamb (Isa. 53:7) and raised as a fish. In order to understand this radical statement, one has to be aware that the sign of the astrological zodiac of the ancient world that was dawning at the time of Jesus was the sign of Pisces, the

Fishes. The itinerant Jewish charismatic was eventually appropriated by the Hellenized culture of the Mediterranean and became the Kyrios, the bearer or lord of the new age.[14] The initials of the phrase "Jesus Christ, Son of God, Savior" spelled out the Greek word ICHTHYS (fish), and soon the persecuted followers of Jesus were tracing the sign of a fish in the sand to identify themselves as members of the new religion.

Within forty years, the literary tradition surrounding Jesus was filled with allusions to fishermen: fishers of men, their nets breaking; the loaves and fishes; the 153 fishes in the net; Peter the fisherman. In spite of recent economic explanations, it is not accidental that Catholics traditionally ate fish on Fridays; for centuries Christianity has been associated with the fish. The astrological Age of Aries, the Ram, had been superseded by that of Jesus Christ, Son of God, the Fish, and the epithets of the former gods were given to him, including "Lord," "Light Bringer," "Shepherd," "Bridegroom," and "faithful Son."

Associations of the nomadic tribes of the patriarchal age with the astrological sign of the Ram have been noted elsewhere. Clearly the numerous references in Hebrew Scripture to the shepherding of their flocks, along with their offering of spotless lambs, reflect a natural part of the nomadic culture of the Hebrew Bible. In the Gospel of John, John the Baptist proclaims Jesus as the Lamb of God. The lamb is the animal commonly offered in the Temple as a sacrifice to Yahweh. John the Baptist greets his cousin with this appellation at their meeting on the banks of the Jordan river (John 2:29). In Isaiah 53, the suffering servant of Yahweh is compared to the lamb led to slaughter. And the image of the butchered lamb is underscored dramatically by the author of Revelation, who refers to Jesus as the Lamb.

After the death of Jesus, the Lamb of God, pious Jews continued to bring their offerings of lambs and turtledoves to the Temple for only four more decades. With the destruction of the Temple of Jerusalem on the ninth of Av, A.D. 70, the practice was terminated. The religion of the Jews could no longer be practiced as prescribed in their sacred Scriptures. We could assume that the Age of Aries was officially over; the Age of Pisces, which Jesus had called "the age to come," had already begun. It might be said that Jesus was the bridge between the two.

I am tempted to believe that the initiates of the first-century wisdom schools of the Roman Empire gradually recognized that in Jesus of Nazareth their ancient myths of the dying and rising god had taken flesh. This belief was the origin of the Christian doctrine of the Incarnation, the birth of the Sun/Son of God—the Logos made flesh. The articulation of this Platonic idea is Greek, not Hebrew. Numerous early Christian writings reflect that Jesus was their "sun of righteousness" and the "light of the world."

Possibly these "enlightened" initiates helped to erect Christianity as a doctrinal system to give continuity to the underlying values of civilization. Chaotic changes and cross-fertilization of cultures created social turmoil during the first century A.D. Clearly, people were seeking a focal point for their "New Age." The institutionalizing of Jesus, the charismatic Jewish Prophet/King, to be the bearer of the astrological Age of Pisces has been alleged to be the work of initiates in the first-century mystery schools. They may even have planned the symbolism for the coming Age of Pisces and its cultural thrust in advance and then watched and waited for someone to be the bearer or "vessel" of these symbols. In any case, they must have recognized in the historical person Jesus of Nazareth a powerful vehicle for the rising age. By naming Jesus "Christos" (Messiah/Anointed) and "Kyrios," they were able to align the popular cult and message of the Jewish miracle-worker with the rising sign of the zodiac, the Fishes.

This mixing of Jewish and Greek influences may seem far-fetched at first glance, but it must be remembered that the area now known as Israel was under Greek hegemony for nearly three hundred years following the conquests of Alexander the Great, and then under Roman occupation after the Roman legions conquered the former Greek provinces. To say that the Jewish mind and culture remained untouched by these centuries of intermingling would be absurd. As one example of this intermingling of cultural influences, a famous sixth-century

Jewish synagogue at Beth Alpha contains a mosaic of the astrological zodiac in its floor—a mosaic with the same symbols as those that flourished in European art in the Middle Ages.

Who was it who first used the initials ICHTHYS to abbreviate the forced Greek epithet "Jesus Christ, Son of God, Savior"? Who first began to use the visual image of the fish to represent Jesus and the Christian movement, a symbol that was very early drawn on the walls of the catacombs outside Rome? Tertullian (who died circa A.D. 230) and Clement of Alexandria (who died in A.D. 215) both used the fish as an appropriate symbol for Jesus, and Saint Augustine continued the practice.[15] Some fathers of the church referred to their parishioners as *pisciculi*, "little fishes."[16] The baptismal font was called *piscina*, and Tertullian says of Christian initiates, "We are born in water like the fish."[17]

The fish/fisherman theme permeates early Christianity, but in the Gospels Jesus never alludes to himself as either fish or fisherman, but rather as shepherd, as bridegroom, and as the heir of the vineyard. It is his Apostles who were designated "fishers of men."

By the latter part of the first century, the image of the fish and the identification of Jesus as the Lord of the Piscean Age permeated Christian doctrine and understanding. The early shared meal of Christians gathered in one another's homes included fish. Many elements of early Christian doctrine and liturgy, particularly its cultic eucharistic meal of bread and wine and its baptismal rites of initiation, can be seen as attempts to reconcile and adapt the historical Jesus, "Son of God," into the Hellenized religious practices borrowed from the mystery cults, particularly those of Tammuz, Mithra, and Dionysius. Naming Jesus "Lord," finally superseding the Roman Emperor, took several centuries, but eventually ICHTHYS, the Fish, was enthroned at the right hand of God as lord of the age.

Whatever the original intent of Jesus might have been, by the time of the writing of the Gospel of John, the Hellenization of the parochial Jewish charismatic was already entrenched. Jesus was not just "Rabbi," as he was known to his friends in Jerusalem, but "Kyrios."

The Gospel of Matthew, written in about A.D. 80–85, already gives grounds for this "lordship" by relating that the astrologers—the Magi or wise men—had "seen his star" (Matt. 2:2). They came from the east and knelt in homage to the newborn King of the Jews.

Modern astrologers suggest that the star of this biblical passage is an allusion to the rising constellation of the Pisces. But here again we encounter the one big flaw in the foundations of Christianity that was overlooked by the early church: the symbol for Pisces is *two* fish swimming together, usually in opposite directions. And the Latin word Pisces is also plural. But in Christianity, instead of two fishes there was only one, Jesus Christ, ICHTHYS, the "only begotten *son*" of God, enthroned at the right hand of the Father. The Bride/Counterpart of this son had been unintentionally lost in the chaotic aftermath of the crucifixion. Perhaps the patriarchs did not realize what damage had been done in deleting the Bride. In any case, when the loss was later made known to them (possibly not until the sixth or seventh century), they must have believed it was too late to reinstate the lost wife of Jesus, whose footprints had been obscured to protect her life.

The Gospels record that Jesus came to fulfill the prophecies of the Jewish nation and to preach a new understanding of God's continuous presence with the community—the poor, the oppressed, and the disenfranchised. The radical content of this message was illustrated when Jesus overturned the moneychangers' tables in the Temple, upsetting the status quo of the elite cult of corrupt priests—"the shepherds who pasture themselves instead of the sheep" (Ezek. 34, Jer. 23). The Jesus described in the Gospel stories is an antiestablishment hero, an incarnation of the spirit of wisdom, gentle and compassionate toward the poor and a champion of justice. It is this Jesus who is the role model for the life of a true Christian.

The Jesus who is victor, ruler, Lord of the Universe, seated at God's right hand, and the object of Christian worship on *Sunday* is a male solar divinity in the Oriental tradition of Egypt (Ra), Greece (Apollo), Rome (Jupiter and Sol Invictus), and Persia (Zoroaster and Mithra).

But there is another Jesus, the charismatic healer who walked the streets of Israel's towns in sandals; who tended the sick and preached a message of reconciliation and relationship; whose baptism was accompanied by the sign of a dove; who was anointed at Bethany and crucified as an insurrectionist by Rome's decree. This is the Jesus who fled whenever the people tried to make him king—and whose death on the cross radically illustrated the woundedness of God, whose prophets are so universally scorned and butchered.

Side by side with the orthodox version of Christianity preached from Peter's chair is another story of Jesus, a hidden tradition that has been branded heretical and forced underground for centuries. In the shadow of the communities that came to believe in a high Christology of Jesus, the heavenly and omnipotent King and Cloud-Rider (an ancient epithet of Baal, the sun god of Canaan), there were those who loved Jesus as brother and friend and who taught a simple gospel of healed relationships and spiritual transformation. The low Christology of the early community of Ebionite Christians shows continuity with the original Jerusalem Christians under the leadership of James, the brother of Jesus.[18] After the teachings of Saint Paul and later church fathers transformed the Jewish rabbi/Messiah into a universal Savior God, the orthodox church eventually (and ironically) labeled the Ebionites heretical![19]

We have examined the beliefs of the alternate tradition, that of the heretical hidden church that taught that Jesus was a spirit-filled charismatic teacher and the Messiah of Israel. It was ultimately my search for this other Jesus that led me to the mystery surrounding the Christian myth of the Holy Grail. And it was my love and reverence for this Jesus that pressed me to speak out for the restoration of his Bride.

The Water Carrier

In light of the fact that the new age of Aquarius is now dawning, it seems fortuitous that the Roman numerals for the year 2000 (and all the years thereafter) are MM and that the initials of Mary Magdalen form the wavy line of the Aquarius sign. In paintings of the Magdalen, her hair is almost invariably shown streaming down her back in the parallel ripples of the sign. I also find it uncanny that in the Cathedral of Chartres, the stained-glass window that depicts Mary Magdalen was donated by the "Water Carriers"; no further information is given.

Who were these medieval Water Carriers? Were they members of a medieval guild in the town? Why did they choose to donate the image of Mary Magdalen rather than that of some other saint? Or is this inscription another cryptic allusion to hope for the restoration of the feminine principle and the Bride in the coming Age of Aquarius? According to the Book of Revelation, it is the marriage of the Lamb that will finally cause water to flow to the desert. The window was installed in the preeminent shrine of the Black Madonna, along with one of the earliest examples of the Jesse Tree (circa 1150), which sprouted in medieval art of this period to emphasize the human genealogy of Jesus in the succession of the kings of Judah.

In one of the fabulous rose windows at Chartres, the baby Jesus on his mother's lap is surrounded by his ancestors—kings of Judah from David's bloodline—again emphasizing the genealogy of the legitimate heirs of David. In this window, the faces of the kings of Israel who "walked with God" and were faithful to him are black, like that of the Madonna holding the Christ Child on her lap. The faces of the kings in the window who ignored God's precepts are white. There is an underlying tenet of medieval artists: "Nothing is without meaning." This is as true of the details in each piece as it is in their fundamental understanding of reality. The "blackness" of these figures seems to refer to the wisdom of those who are willing servants of God.

The Little Mermaid

A seven-year-old friend of mine named Sarah pointed out to me a curious anomaly in the early minutes of the Disney film *The Little Mermaid*. The painting that the little fish-girl Ariel had salvaged from a shipwrecked galleon and kept among her treasures was *The Penitent Magdalen,* by the seventeenth-century French artist Georges de la Tour. The Disney movie is adapted from the original version of the story written by Hans Christian Andersen, but the film has a revised happy ending—the marriage of the prince and his bride. The Little Mermaid's one desire is to rise from the ocean and to marry the prince. Perhaps she represents the *second* fish of the sign of Pisces, the one forgotten and misplaced, submerged in our unconscious for two thousand years!

Both the evil sea witch and Ariel's own benevolent father, King Poseidon, try to prevent her union with the prince. The sea witch conspires to steal her voice, making her unable to communicate with the prince. (Was not "the voice of the Bride" stolen when her story was declared heretical and her marriage repudiated?) Once again, the motif of the fairy tale is the feminine rising from the depths of obscurity to fulfill her destiny as true partner to the masculine. And, again, it is the prince who is in the deepest trouble, shipwrecked and near death when Ariel saves him during the storm. It is also the prince, desperately searching for his lost Sister-Bride, who is cruelly duped by the evil sea witch. His sad plight is his separation from his beloved.

But I have a question: Who chose the picture of *The Penitent Magdalen* to hang in the Little Mermaid's treasure cave in the Disney movie? Was it the artist's conscious association of the mermaid with the Magdalen? Or was it just a coincidence, another potent synchronicity?

An even weightier question is posed by the choice of the name Ariel chosen for the Little Mermaid, who is not named in Andersen's version. For Ariel is another name for Jerusalem, used in the book of the prophet Isaiah as a synonym for the "city besieged" (Isa. 29:1–2). It is the symbolic equivalent of the "desolated widow Sion" from Lamentations and the "Magdal-eder" from Micah 4:8. Ariel represents the abandoned remnant of the people of God. Perhaps the choice of the name was unconscious on the part of the storyteller, but it speaks volumes. Ariel's true identity is that of the Lost Bride. The "fish maiden" is seeking to be brought into our consciousness as the companion/ counterpart of the handsome prince. The sign of the passing Age of Pisces is *two* fish, not one! Swimming in opposite directions, the astrological sign of the Fishes looks very much like the yin/yang of the Orient, ancient symbol for the harmony of the opposites.

In the watermarks of Provence, the mermaid holds in her hand the mirror of Venus/Aphrodite, the love goddess, her alter ego. I believe that this mirror, which appears in several Georges de la Tour paintings of *The Penitent Magdalen* (and also in the first panel of *La Dame à la Licorne* tapestry), reflects the understanding that the material cosmos, embodied in the feminine (*matter* comes from Latin *mater*, meaning "mother"), is the mirror image of divinity and is understood to be the "other half" or counterpart of the spiritual. It is the physical world that manifests the unseen creative energy of the universe "in the flesh." In this sense, the material cosmos (feminine in the ancient cosmologies) "catches the spirit" in her mirror and holds it there, making it visible, as the ocean reflects the wholeness of the sky or the moon the light of the sun. Perhaps this explains why the love goddess is associated with a mirror. It is certainly not because she is vain; it is because she is the mirror image of the unseen positive energy of the cosmos.

The little mermaid with the mirror in the Disney movie is a diminutive of the Queen of the Sea, the archetypal Goddess. But she is not a mother image; she represents the "other Mary," the Sister-Bride. The folk have a strange way of telling their tales in archetypal forms. Perhaps we should show no surprise when these forms recur!

Restoring the Lost Bride

In restoring the feminine principle embodied in Mary Magdalen, it is necessary to establish her true identity as Bride rather than prostitute. The real Mary Magdalen, although later called prostitute by the church, was never scorned by Jesus in the Gospels. She was the love of his life. As in the fairy tales, the handsome prince has been seeking her for two thousand years, trying to restore her to her rightful place at his side. He represents the Shepherd/Bridegroom aspect of the deity; she represents the Bride: "No longer shall you be called 'forsaken" and your lands 'desolate,' but you shall be called 'my beloved' and your lands 'espoused'" (Isa. 62:4).

After nearly two thousand years, it is time to set the record straight, to revise and complete the Gospel story of Jesus to include his wife. Our ravaged environment, our abused children, our maimed veterans, our self-destructing families and abandoned spouses are all crying for the restoration of the Bride of Christ. Perhaps their anguish is best summed up in the image of the Madonna who cries. Numerous icons of the Madonna have been given media coverage in recent years; they shed tears, defying rational explanation. Surely she is grieving for her children, the *anawim* of God.

The Scriptures never said that Jesus was not married; they only omitted specific mention of his wife. But, as we have seen, the physical danger to his family would have been reason enough to blot Jesus' marriage from the record. Suffice it to remember that his beloved sat at his feet drinking in his every word (Luke 10:39) and that she anointed his feet with her tears and dried them with her hair (John 12:3). The archetypal Bride is already in place, and a new consciousness is taking root among us. The voice of the Bride is at last being heard in the land.

When I first set out to debunk the Grail heresy in 1985, I had no idea where my journey would lead. In my synthesis of evidence from history, art, literature, psychology, and mythology, the arguments for the existence of the Lost Bride gradually crystallized. Everywhere I found traces of the lost feminine and the imbalance of opposites that manifests in the image of the wasteland, the crippled king, and the broken-hearted Madonna.

In my search for the Grail, I encountered myths and legends from many lands. One that was particularly enchanting was the ancient Egyptian rendering of the goddess Maat. Often she is depicted as a giant bird who holds the entire world in perfect balance, while at the same time holding a feather with which she could tip the scales to one side or the other. Not wishing to have the universe become unbalanced, she continues to hold that single feather for all eternity.

Unfortunately, over the last four millennia on our planet, the scales have been tipped in favor of the masculine, causing the equilibrium to be destroyed at all levels. For millennia, prophets and the truly wise have exhorted the community to be compassionate, merciful, and gracious, even as God expresses these qualities. In this new era, perhaps the water-carrying principle, the feminine, will have enough influence to put out the fires kindled by two thousand years of male Logos orientation and to begin to heal the desert. It is clearly a matter of a new consciousness. When the Sister-Bride is restored to the celestial paradigm as the Beloved of Logos, then the woundedness will be healed; for as we have seen, the source of the wound is the alienation and separation of these two archetypes.

Medieval legends say that the Grail was lost because its custodians proved unworthy. Gradually, both the Catholic Church and the hidden Church of Love became so involved in the power struggle, so "blade" oriented, so eager to be declared the ultimate ruler and the chosen vehicle of God's message, that they lost the message itself. The hierarchy of each cause, in its insistence on its own version of the myth of "chosenness," believed that it was the favored one, the only true instrument of God's will. Each faction employed the sword of ruthless power politics to attain its goals and in so doing managed to destroy the very message it carried. That message was love. In the end, neither was able to hear the Word of God over the clashes of their swords.

Now the feminine is rising to carry the message. Like Briar Rose, finally awakened by the kiss of her prince, she is now able to articulate the message of Eros/relatedness. The bloodline issue is basically irrelevant, except as it applies to the question of the full humanity of Jesus. But the resurrected feminine consciousness will continue to move toward equal partnership in spite of the myth of the dominant male that has been perpetrated for millennia.

It is not clear what the patriarchal establishment of Christianity will do when it is discovered that the legends of the Lost Bride of Jesus are probably true. It is possible that the Vatican will continue to deny that Jesus was married. But it is also possible, when faced with the evidence, that the fathers will decide it is time to receive the Bride in joyful thanksgiving. Perhaps they will allow the church bells to ring out across the land to announce her safe return and to welcome her home! They might be moved to celebrate at last the wedding supper of the Lamb. Then the voices of the Bride and Bridegroom will again be heard in the land, and the desert *shall* bloom!

> The desert and the parched land will exult,
> the steppe will rejoice and bloom.
>
> —Isa. 35:1

THE SACRED REUNION

Shrouded in mists of time
she waits alone in the garden,
veiled, her name obscured,
the forsaken Rose.
Lost counterpart of Logos, the Word,
Son of the Father,
reason and righteousness,
the eternal He.
Forgotten Eros,
the passionate one,
the eternal She,
left prostrate on the ground.

"The Bride is as dark—
but lovely—
as the tents of Cedar.
Do not stare at her because she is swarthy,
because the sun has burned her.
She has labored in her brothers' vineyards;
her own she has not kept." (Cant. 1:5–6)

The Bride,
parched from her toil
in the scorching sun,
dark, dried, and withered.
Black Madonna,

mother of the afflicted poor,
God's raisins,
burned in the relentless rays
of Logos, victor, judge, and sword.
Male image of a sovereign God
raised to heaven's throne—
alone.

Eagerly she sought him,
but watchmen came upon her,
struck and wounded her,
the guardians of the walls.
Her plight is mirrored now
in Czestochowa's icon,
a gash upon her cheek,
the abused, abandoned one—
the Derelicta.

Noli me tangere:
"Do not touch me."
For centuries the echo:
Noli me tangere.

The Ascended One,
adored and glorified—
untouchable,
the handsome prince,
Lion of Judah and Lamb of God
seated at the Father's hand
and ruling from his throne—
alone.

But now, at last, he seeks her.
He calls for her.
He knows the name of the Rose.

Exhausted and parched
in wretchedness,
she hears him call her name.
She stirs, raises her head, and looks around.
"Who speaks?"

Her heart beats faster.
"Can it be he?
Has he returned at last for me?"

The garden where he left her
is now a wasteland—
scarred, dried, and shriveled.
Trees are stunted,
streams of living water
only a trickle.
Thickets of thorn
surround the garden,
barring his way.
With the sword of truth
he must hack them to pieces
to reach his beloved.

At last he finds her,
still clasping her alabaster jar.
Her joyful tears fall at his feet.
A second time she dries them with her hair.
But now he reaches for her hand.
"Come, beloved; it is time.
Let us go together into the vineyard
to see if the vines are in bloom." (Cant. 7:13)
Hand in hand now,
they walk in the desert garden.
And where their feet tread
a violet springs up from the ground,

an anemone lifts its head.
In their wake
buds swell on barren bough.
"No longer will you be called 'forsaken'
and your lands 'desolate,'
but you shall be called 'beloved,'
and your lands 'espoused.'" (Isa. 62:4)

He whispers her name,
savoring its taste
delighting in the Bride of his longing.

Mary.

N O T E S

CHAPTER I

1. Michael Baigent, Richard Leigh, and Henry Lincoln, *Holy Blood, Holy Grail* (New York: Little, Brown & Co., 1983), 286. First published as *The Holy Blood and the Holy Grail* (London: Jonathan Cape, Ltd., 1982).

2. Arthur E. Waite, *The Hidden Church of the Holy Grail* (London: Rebman, Ltd., 1909).

3. Baigent, Leigh, and Lincoln, 306.

4. Edith Filliette, *Saint Mary Magdalene, Her Life and Times* (Newton Lower Falls, MA: Society of Saint Mary Magdalene, 1983), 39.

5. Harold Bayley, *The Lost Language of Symbolism* (Totowa, NJ: Rowman & Littlefield, 1974), vol. 1, 168–177. First published Great Britain: Williams and Norgate, 1912.

6. Marjorie M. Malvern, *Venus in Sackcloth* (Edwardsville, IL: University of Southern Illinois Press, 1974).

CHAPTER II

1. Merlin Stone, *When God Was a Woman* (New York: The Dial Press, 1976), xii.

2. Jonathan Smith, "Wisdom and Apocalyptic," in *Visionaries and Their Apocalypses*, ed. Paul D. Hanson (Philadelphia: Fortress Press, 1983), 104.

3. James Barclay, *The Mind of Jesus* (New York: Harper & Row, 1960), 186.

4. Elisabeth Schüssler Fiorenza, *In Memory of Her* (New York: Crossroads, 1988), xiv.

5. F. Edward Hulme, *Symbolism in Christian Art* (London: Swan, Sonnenschein & Co., 1891), 200.

6. Barclay, 198.

7. Ibid.

8. Marvin H. Pope, *Song of Songs, Anchor Bible Series* (Garden City, NY: Doubleday & Co., 1983), 19.

9. Ibid.

10. Samuel Kramer, *The Sacred Marriage Rite* (Bloomington, IN: University of Indiana Press, 1969), 88.

11. Helmer Ringgren, *Religions of the Ancient Near East*, trans. John Sturdy (Philadelphia: Westminster Press, 1973), 11, 42.

12. Ibid., 101.

13. Ibid. Chapter 1, pp. 1–48, contains a detailed discussion and poetic passages from these Sumerian rituals.

14. See Raphael Patai, *The Hebrew Goddess* (Hoboken, NJ: KTAV Publishing House, 1967) for a complete discussion of the apostasy of the Jewish nation.

15. Bayley, 169.

16. David R. Cartlidge and David L. Dungan, *Documents for Study of the Gospels* (Philadelphia: Fortress Press, 1980), 61. A very brief discussion of Gnostic understanding and practice of the symbolic "sacred marriage" and the "bridal chamber."

17. Denis de Rougemont, *Love in the Western World*, trans. Montgomery Belgion (New York: Pantheon Books, 1956), 21.

CHAPTER III

1. Robert Graves, *King Jesus* (New York: Farrar, Straus and Giroux, Minerva Press, 1946), 293.

2. Alexander Cruden, *Cruden's Unabridged Concordance* (Grand Rapids, MI: Baker Book House, 1973), 582.

3. James Robinson, ed., *The Nag Hammadi Library* (San Francisco: Harper & Row, 1988). This volume contains translations of both of these Gnostic Gospels in English.

4. Ibid., "The Gospel of Philip," 135–136.

5. Ibid., 138.

6. S.G.F. Brandon, *Jesus and the Zealots* (New York: Charles Scribner's Sons, 1967).

7. Ibid., 39.

8. Ibid.

9. Ibid., 344.

10. Jean Daniélou, *The Dead Sea Scrolls and Primitive Christianity*, trans. Salvator Attanasio (New York: New American Library, 1962), 106.

11. Morton Smith, *Jesus the Magician* (New York: Harper & Row, 1978).

12. Brandon, 294.

13. Baigent, Leigh, and Lincoln, 107.

14. Hulme, 29.

15. Ibid.

CHAPTER IV

1. Baigent, Leigh, and Lincoln, 394.

2. Ibid., 114.

3. Ibid., 268.

4. Zoé Oldenbourg, *The Massacre at Montségur*, trans. Peter Green (New York: Pantheon Books, 1961), 42.

5. Ibid.

6. The alleged Merovingian genealogies of the Priory of Sion are published in Michael Baigent, Richard Leigh, and Henry Linoln, *The Holy Blood and the Holy Grail* (London: Jonathan Cape, Ltd., 1982).

7. Frederick Goldin, trans., *Lyrics of the Troubadours and Trouvères* (Garden City, NY: Anchor Books, Doubleday & Co., 1973), 217.

8. Wayland Young, *Eros Denied* (New York: Grove Press, 1964), 210.

9. de Rougemont, 85.

10. Meg Bogin, *The Women Troubadours* (New York: Paddington Press, 1976), 58.

11. Baigent, Leigh, and Lincoln, 395.

12. Louis Charpentier, *The Mysteries of Chartres Cathedral.* (Northhamptonshire: Thorsons Publishers Ltd., 1972).

13. Ibid., 147.

14. Fred Gettings, *The Secret Zodiac* (London: Routledge & Kegan Paul, 1987).

15. Henry Lincoln, *The Holy Place* (New York: Brown & Little, Arcade Books, 1991), 69.

16. Barclay, 9.

17. Patai, 178.

CHAPTER V

1. All watermarks referred to in this chapter are taken from Harold Bayley, *The Lost Language of Symbolism* (Totowa, NJ: Rowman & Littlefield, 1974).

2. Bayley, vol. 1, p. 1.

3. Ibid., 26.

4. Ibid., 120.

5. Cruden, 582.

6. Richard Cavendish, *The Tarot* (New York: Crescent Books, 1975), 17.

7. Baigent, Leigh, and Lincoln, 217, 219.

8. Ibid., 159.

9. Ibid., 131.

10. Lincoln, 69.

CHAPTER VI

1. Michael Levey and Gabriele Mandel, *Complete Paintings of Botticelli* (New York: Viking Penguin, Inc., 1985), 109. First published in Italy: Rizzoli Editore, 1967.

2. Baigent, Leigh, and Lincoln, 131.

3. Arthur E. Waite, *A New Encyclopaedia of Freemasonry* (New York: Weathervane Books, 1970), vol. 2, p. 455.

4. Baigent, Leigh, and Lincoln, 159.

5. Robert Graves, *The White Goddess* (New York: Farrar, Straus & Giroux, 1966), 472.

6. See John Michell, *The Dimensions of Paradise* (San Francisco: Harper & Row, 1990). First published in London: Thames and Hudson, Ltd., 1988.

7. Michael Baigent and Richard Leigh, *The Temple and the Lodge* (New York: Little, Brown & Co., 1989). This book elucidates the presence of the Knights Templar in Scotland.

CHAPTER VII

1. Alain Erlande-Brandenburg, *La Dame à la Licorne* (Paris: Éditions de la Réunion des Musées Nationaux, 1979), 67.

2. Ibid., 66.

3. Ibid., 13–59. Alain Erlande-Brandenburg, the curator of the Cluny Museum, interprets the first five panels of the tapestry as representing each of the five senses.

4. John Williamson, *The Oak King, the Holly King, and the Unicorn* (New York: Harper & Row, 1986), 199–226.

5. Ibid.

6. Kramer, 63.

7. Williamson. Williamson identifies each plant in the tapestry panel along with its medieval significance.

CHAPTER VIII

1. de Rougemont, 111.

2. Ibid., 82.

3. See Zsolt Aradi, *Shrines of Our Lady around the World* (New York: Farrar, Straus & Young, 1954), for descriptions and details of shrines of the Black Madonna in Europe.

4. Bernard of Clairvaux, *On the Song of Songs*, trans. Kilian Walsh (Kalamazoo, MI: Cistercian Publications, 1976), "Sermon 25," 56–57.

CHAPTER IX

1. Herbert Silberer, *Hidden Symbolism of Alchemy and the Occult Arts* (New York: Dover Publications, 1971), 399.

2. Riane Eisler, *The Chalice and the Blade* (San Francisco: Harper & Row, 1988), 72.

3. Ibid.

4. Barbara Walker, *Woman's Dictionary of Symbols and Sacred Objects* (San Francisco: Harper & Row, 1988), 69.

5. Marie-Louise von Franz, *Alchemy* (Toronto: Inner City Books, 1980), 62.

6. Ibid., 65.

7. Ibid., 180–181. Marie-Louise von Franz relates this story of Saint Thomas Aquinas.

8. Silberer, 187.

9. Ibid., 399.

10. Patai, 178.

11. Ibid.

12. Samuel Terrien, *The Golden Bible Atlas* (New York: The Golden Press, 1957), 73.

13. Cruden, 582.

14. Michell. Michell discusses the secret wisdom of classical antiquity, including the canon of sacred number and the influence of this ancient wisdom tradition in the formation of Christianity as a religion of the Roman Empire.

15. Hulme, 203.

16. Ibid., 204.

17. Ibid., 205.

18. Brandon, 217.

19. Ibid.

S E L E C T E D
B I B L I O G R A P H Y

Aradi, Zsolt. *Shrines of Our Lady around the World.* New York: Farrar, Straus & Young, 1954.

Baigent, Michael, and Richard Leigh. *The Temple and the Lodge.* New York: Little, Brown & Co., 1989.

Baigent, Michael, Richard Leigh, and Henry Lincoln. *The Holy Blood and the Holy Grail.* London: Jonathan Cape, Ltd., 1982. Reprinted as *Holy Blood, Holy Grail.* New York: Dell Publishing Co., 1983.

Barclay, James. *The Mind of Jesus.* New York: Harper & Row, 1960.

Bayley, Harold. *The Lost Language of Symbolism.* Totowa, NJ: Rowman & Littlefield, 1974. First published by Williams and Norgate, 1912.

Bernard of Clairvaux. *On the Song of Songs.* Translated by Kilian Walsh, OCSO. Kalamazoo, MI: Cistercian Publications, Inc., 1983.

Bogin, Meg. *The Women Troubadours.* New York: Paddington Press, 1976.

Brandon, S.G.F. *Jesus and the Zealots.* New York: Charles Scribner's Sons, 1967.

Briquet, Charles-Moïse. *Les Filigranes.* Edited by Allan Stevenson. In *The New Briquet, Jubilee Edition*, general ed. J. S. G. Simmons (Amsterdam: The Paper Publications Society, 1968), vol. iii, iv.

Brown, Raymond E. *The Community of the Beloved Disciple.* New York: Paulist Press, 1979.

———, ed. *The Jerome Biblical Commentary.* New Jersey: Prentice Hall, 1968.

Cartlidge, David R., and David L. Dungan, eds. *Documents for Study of the Gospels.* Philadelphia: Fortress Press, 1980.

Cavendish, Richard. *The Tarot.* London: M. Joseph, Ltd., 1975. Reprint. New York: Crescent Books, 1986.

Charpentier, Louis. *The Mysteries of Chartres Cathedral.* Translated by Ronald Fraser and Janette Jackson. Northhamptonshire: Thorsons Publishers Ltd., 1972.

Cruden, Alexander. *Cruden's Unabridged Concordance*. Grand Rapids, MI: Baker Book House, 1973.

Danielou, Jean. *The Dead Sea Scrolls and Primitive Christianity*. Translated by Salvator Attanasio. New York: New American Library, Mentor Omega Book, 1962.

de Rougemont. *See* Rougemont, Denis de.

Eisler, Riane. *The Chalice and the Blade*. San Francisco: Harper & Row, 1988.

Erlande-Brandenburg, Alain. *La Dame à la Licorne*. Paris: Éditions de la Réunion des Musées Nationaux, 1970.

Filliette, Edith. *Saint Mary Magdalene, Her Life and Times*. Newton Lower Falls, MA: Society of Saint Mary Magdalene, 1983.

Fiorenza, Elisabeth Schüssler. *The Book of Revelation: Justice and Judgment*. Philadelphia: Fortress Press, 1984.

———. *In Memory of Her*. New York: Crossroads, 1988.

Franz, Marie-Louise von. *Alchemy*. Toronto: Inner City Books, 1980.

Fujita, Niel S. *The Crack in the Jar*. New York: Paulist Press, 1986.

Gettings, Fred. *The Secret Zodiac*. London: Routledge & Kegan Paul, 1987.

Goldin, Frederick, trans. *Lyrics of the Troubadours and Trouvères*. Garden City, NY: Anchor Books, Doubleday & Co., 1973.

Graves, Robert. *King Jesus*. New York: Farrar, Straus & Giroux, 1946.

———. *The White Goddess*. New York: Farrar, Straus & Giroux, 1966.

Hamilton, Edith. *Mythology*. New York: New American Library, Mentor Book, 1969.

Holy Bible. New International Version. New York: The American Bible Society, 1978.

Hulme, F. Edward. *Symbolism in Christian Art*. London: Swan, Sonnenschein & Co., 1891. Reprint. Detroit: Gale Research Co., 1969.

Inman, Thomas. *Ancient Pagan and Modern Christian Symbolism*. Published 1884. Reprint. Williamstown, MA: Corner House Publishers, 1978.

Kramer, Samuel. *The Sacred Marriage Rite*. Bloomington, IN: Indiana University Press, 1969.

Levey, Michael, and Gabriele Mandel. *Complete Paintings of Botticelli*. New York: Penguin Classics of World Art, Viking Penguin, Inc., 1985.

Lincoln, Henry. *The Holy Place.* New York: Brown & Little, Arcade Books, 1991.

Malvern, Marjorie M. *Venus in Sackcloth.* Edwardsville, IL: Southern Illinois University Press, 1975.

Michell, John. *The City of Revelation.* London: Garnstone Press, 1971.

———. *The Dimensions of Paradise.* San Francisco: Harper & Row, 1990.

Oldenbourg, Zoé. *Massacre at Montségur.* Translated by Peter Green. New York: Pantheon Books, 1961.

Pagels, Elaine. *The Gnostic Gospels.* New York: Vintage Books, 1981.

Patai, Raphael. *The Hebrew Goddess.* Hoboken, NJ: KTAV Publishing House, 1967.

Perrin, Norman. *The Resurrection According to Matthew, Mark and Luke.* Philadelphia: Fortress Press, 1960.

Pilch, John J. *What Are They Saying about the Book of Revelation?* New York: Paulist Press, 1978.

Pope, Marvin H. *Song of Songs.* Anchor Bible Series. Garden City: Doubleday & Co., Inc., 1983.

Qualls-Corbett, Nancy. *The Sacred Prostitute.* Toronto: Inner City Books, 1988.

Ringgren, Helmer. *The Faith of Qumran.* Translated by Emilie T. Sander. Philadelphia: Fortress Press, 1963.

———. *Religions of the Ancient Near East.* Translated by John Sturdy. Philadelphia: Westminster Press, 1973.

Robinson, James M., ed. *The Nag Hammadi Library.* San Francisco: Harper & Row, 1981.

Rougemont, Denis de. *Love in the Western World.* Translated by Montgomery Belgion. New York: Pantheon Books, 1956.

Saint Joseph New Catholic Edition of the Holy Bible. New York: Catholic Book Publishing Company, 1963.

Schick, Edwin A. *Revelation, the Last Book of the Bible.* Philadelphia: Fortress Press, 1977.

Schonfield, Hugh. *The Pentecost Revolution.* Dorset: Element Books, 1985.

Silberer, Herbert. *Hidden Symbolism of Alchemy and the Occult Arts.* New York: Moffat, Yard & Co., 1917. Reprint. New York: Dover Publications, 1971.

Smith, Jonathan. "Wisdom and Apocalyptic." In *Visionaries and their Apocalypses*, edited by P.D. Hanson. Philadelphia: Fortress Press, 1988.

Smith, Morton. *Jesus the Magician*. San Francisco: Harper & Row, 1978.

_____. *The Secret Gospel*. New York: Harper and Row, 1973.

Sparks, H.F.D., ed. *The Apocryphal Old Testament*. New York: Oxford University Press, 1984.

Stone, Merlin. *When God Was a Woman*. New York: The Dial Press, 1976.

Terrien, Samuel. *The Golden Bible Atlas*. New York: The Golden Press, 1957.

Vermes, G. *The Dead Sea Scrolls in English*. New York: Penguin Books, 1987.

von Franz. *See* Franz, Marie-Louise von.

Waite, Arthur E. *The Hidden Church of the Holy Grail*. London: Rebman Limited, 1909.

_____. *The New Encyclopaedia of Freemasonry*. New York: Weathervane Books, 1970.

Walker, Barbara. *The Woman's Dictionary of Symbols and Sacred Objects*. San Francisco: Harper & Row, 1988.

_____. *The Woman's Encyclopedia of Myths and Secrets*. San Francisco: Harper & Row, 1983.

Williamson, John. *The Oak King, the Holly King, and the Unicorn*. New York: Harper & Row, 1986.

Young, Wayland. *Eros Denied*. New York: Grove Press, 1964.

I N D E X

ABOUT THE AUTHOR

Margaret Starbird has done graduate study in European history and comparative literature, and holds a master of arts degree from the University of Maryland. She has studied at Christian Albrechts Universität in Kiel, Germany, where she was a Fulbright Fellow, and at Vanderbilt University Divinity School in Nashville, Tennessee. Margaret has taught numerous classes in Scripture study and spirituality. She has traveled extensively in Europe and has lived in Japan and in various parts of the United States. She and her husband now reside in the Puget Sound area of Washington; they have five children.

"Already as a small child," she says, "I believed that when the Holy Grail was found, it would heal the 'wasteland.' That was the promise of the Arthurian legends my mother read to me." In this book, the author shows how the feminine was, however inadvertently, dropped from the Christian story, why its loss has had such a devastating negative impact on Western civilization, and how it can be restored. The book articulates her own search for the Holy Grail.

BOOKS OF RELATED INTEREST

THE GODDESS IN THE GOSPELS
Reclaiming the Sacred Feminine
by Margaret Starbird

THE GOSPEL OF MARY MAGDALENE
by Jean-Yves Leloup

THE SECRET BOOKS OF THE EGYPTIAN GNOSTICS
by Jean Doresse

THE TEMPLARS AND THE ASSASSINS
The Militia of Heaven
by James Wasserman

CHRIST THE YOGI
A Hindu Reflection on the Gospel of John
by Ravi Ravindra, Ph.D.

THE WAY OF THE ESSENES
Christ's Hidden Life Remembered
by Anne and Daniel Meurois-Givaudan

THE PATH OF THE PRIESTESS
A Guidebook for Awakening the Divine Feminine
by Sharron Rose

THE WAY OF HERMES
New Translations of *The Corpus Hermeticum* and
The Definitions of Hermes Trismegistus to Asclepius
Translated by Clement Salaman, Dorine van Oyen, William D.
Wharton, and Jean-Pierre Mahé

Inner Traditions • Bear & Company
P.O. Box 388
Rochester, VT 05767
1-800-246-8648
www.InnerTraditions.com
Or contact your local bookseller